AF380353

As believers, we find ourselves wading neck deep in a culture flooded with lies and misinformation. This false narrative comes from Satan himself, whom Scripture calls the "god of this world" and the "prince of the power of the air." Even the Lord Himself referred to the devil as the "father of lies" (John 8:44). Because of this, we must always be anchored to the truth found in God's word. In his new book, *The Devil's Newsroom: Muting Satan's Fake News and Tuning in to God's Truth*, my friend Jeff Schreve does a masterful job of exposing Satan's deceptions and equipping believers with the truth they need to combat these last-days lies. As you read, your faith will be recharged and readied to move forward with confidence and courage!

—JEFF KINLEY
Bible Teacher and Host, The King is Coming

Terms like "misinformation," "censorship," "propaganda," and "fake news" are so overused in the media today that we've lost the understanding of just how important Truth (with a capital "T") really is. That's why Jeff Schreve's new book is so important. It doesn't just expose what's actually happening, but it ties today's censorship culture to what the Bible says about living a transparent life. Every Christian needs to read this book and use it as a guide to understand the difference between what today's culture *says*, and what it really *means*. In many ways, our future depends on it.

—PHIL COOKE, PH.D.
Media Producer, Media Consultant, Founder of Cooke Media Group, and Author of *Church on Trial: How to Protect Your Congregation, Mission, and Reputation During a Crisis.*

The Bible reveals to us God's good news. It's the greatest news in all the world because believing it will result in receiving eternal life through the Lord Jesus Christ. When the message that brings salvation gets denied or distorted then the hope of salvation is hidden from sight. That's what makes fake news so deadly. I am grateful that Jeff Schreve has exercised his insights and pastoral wisdom to show us how the Bible itself warns us against fake news. *The Devil's Newsroom* will help you recognize and resist being taken astray by false gospels so that you might come to know, believe, and grow in the good news that forgives sin and reconciles to God.

—DR. THOMAS ASCOL
Pastor, Author, and President of Founders Ministries

When fake news masquerades as good news, the Gospel is under attack and our grandkids are in jeopardy. Jeff's book is a whistle-blower, exposing the deception of false gospels, refreshing us with biblical truth.

—KIRK CAMERON
Actor, Evangelist, TV Host, and Founder of American Campfire Revival

"Jeff Schreve is one of the most knowledgeable voices speaking about the intersections of faith and culture, the distortions of facts present in news coverage each day, and the spiritual state of our world. I urge people to read *The Devil's Newsroom: Muting Satan's Fake News and Tuning in to God's Truth.* Schreve's research will grip your heart and equip your mind; his work will motivate you to pray for the opening of the eyes of people that God still loves very much—the widely misled, largely prodigal multitudes all around us known as "Americans."

Experience the book *The Devil's Newsroom,* and meet my valued colleague, brother, and friend, Jeff Schreve."

—ALEX MCFARLAND
Christian Apologist, Theologian, Author, Speaker, Radio Host

Recently a good friend and member of our church spoke with me about his frustration with preachers "Who can't throw a strike." If you know baseball, you know how important it is for the pitcher to throw strikes rather than constantly throwing pitches out of the strike zone. Bases on balls will wreck a game and the team's ability to win. Unfortunately, too many preachers are wild and all over the place, nibbling around the strike zone with soft stuff, curve balls, and missing the zone with nuances. Jeff Schreve knows how to "throw strikes." As a faithful, effective pastor, he preaches the Word of God with clarity and conviction. And no one has to wonder where he stands on the key issues of Christian faith and living. *The Devil's Newsroom* exposes the lies of Satan with God's Word and with bold conviction, profound wisdom, and pastoral counsel from a true man of God. We live in critical times when truth is under attack and godless secularism is on the rise. The lies of the Enemy are louder than ever. In order to change the direction of a culture, we must confront the lies we hear every day with God's Truth and Good News. We must arm ourselves with the Word of God and declare the one true message of hope in Jesus Christ. Christians in the twenty-first century must be willing to fight for what is right in an era of deception. So much is at stake. There is no neutrality or nuance in this spiritual battle which is raging all around us. May God give us courageous faith to confront this age with a bold defense of truth. The price of being fearful or fuzzy on the issues of our times is too great. Let us who follow Jesus be clear, convictional, and courageous. The enemies of truth are relentless, and the lies keep coming. Let us "earnestly contend for the faith" which is once delivered to the saints (Jude 3).

The book you are about to read will help prepare you to live your faith and point you to a genuine love for Jesus who is the reason we fight for our faith, our families, and our future. God bless you, Jeff Schreve, for throwing strikes!

—DR. JACK GRAHAM
Pastor, Founder of PowerPoint Ministries, Speaker and Author

To have victory in the spiritual realm we must know our enemy. Jeff Schreve gives his readers a true profile of the enemy and how we can defeat the evil one who truly does sit on a throne of lies.

—TIM WILDMON
President of American Family Association

Scripture poses the question in Isaiah 53:1, "Who has believed our report?" Pastor Jeff Schreve's new book *The Devil's Newsroom* makes clear that the report of the lame stream media in America should not be believed. It is no exaggeration to say that they traffic in lies, which is Satan's stock in trade. Jeff exposes their grand deception with clarity and cogency that every American should take to heart. Jesus said in John 8:32, " . . . You shall know the truth and the truth shall make you free." God's truth liberates. Satan's lies enslave. If you love truth and hate lies, you'll love this book. Pastor Schreve inspires us to always believe God's report, not "the Devil's newsroom."

—BISHOP E. W. JACKSON
President of S.T.A.N.D (Staying True to American's National Destiny),
Pastor, Attorney, and Marine Corps Veteran

THE DEVIL'S NEWS ROOM

Muting Satan's Fake News & Tuning in to God's Truth

Dr. Jeff Schreve

Table of Contents

Foreword

Jeff Schreve is one of the most gifted biblical communicators in America. He serves as the beloved and respected pastor of the First Baptist Church of Texarkana, but his wide-reaching television and radio ministry extends his influence far beyond his church's pulpit.

His latest book *The Devil's Newsroom: Muting Satan's Fake News and Tuning in to God's Truth* is a timely and insightful reminder that our real battle in the culture of our day is not political, but spiritual. Sure, the results of this spiritual battle is reflected in the politics of the day, but that is the manifestation of what's really the underbelly of a culture that has forsaken a Judeo-Christian foundation for the false flag pushed by the demonic forces of the Devil.

It's no small wonder that many people, including millions who declare themselves to be Christians, have followed lies about the authority of Scripture, human sexuality, gender identity, the importance of Israel, the sanctity of human life, and the role of marriage. We are way beyond correcting these errors by politely and gently reminding church members to attend service more often. As Jeff Schreve illustrates, it's time to take the firehose to the flames coming from the pits of hell in the form of the "fake news" masquerading as a "new and improved Christian message."

The historical biblical record was, is, and will forever be the standard by which we will be measured and it's so refreshing to witness the conviction with which Jeff Schreve applies the Word of God to the issues of today. His bold, uncompromised, and yet compassionate approach is refreshing in its clarity and restorative in its construct.

I hope you are as blessed by the message and ministry of Jeff Schreve as I am. He is one of our country's most important Christian voices. As you read this book, you will understand why I feel this way!

—MIKE HUCKABEE

US Ambassador to Israel, Former Governor of Arkansas, Author, Speaker, TV Host

Introduction

When I was a kid, *Perry Mason* was one of my father's favorite television shows. My dad loved the well-orchestrated suspense of this classic legal drama. In every episode, defense lawyer extraordinaire Perry Mason represented a defendant who appeared to be guilty as sin. But as we all know, appearances can be deceiving. In the final moments of each program, the truth prevailed. The circumstantial evidence against Mason's client, evidence that seemed so ironclad, would crumble under the weight of facts, logic, cross-examination, and the smitten conscience of the real perpetrator.

While watching *Perry Mason* with my dad, I learned an important question that was and is standard operating procedure for any witness in a court of law: "Do you swear to tell the truth, the whole truth, and nothing but the truth, so help you God?" You see, for the judicial system to operate correctly, witnesses must be compelled to tell the truth. The truth matters greatly in court, just as it does in every aspect of life. If you don't have truth, you don't have anything. Marriages, families, relationships, businesses, churches, societies, and the souls of men are literally ruined and destroyed by lies and falsehoods.

The Bible is God's word of truth and the foundation for faith and practice. From the Scriptures, we learn that Jesus is God's only Son and man's only Savior. He is deity in the flesh and the embodiment and personification of truth. The Bible also teaches that the devil is the archenemy of truth and the one who deceives the whole world. He "never ceases to make crooked the straight ways of the Lord" (Acts 13:10). From the time Satan rebelled against God in heaven, he has been the master liar and the chief propagator of fake news. His lies to mankind began in the Garden of Eden (Genesis 3), and they continue to this day. Without exaggeration, the devil lives to deceive.

Have you been deceived by the deceiver? So many people in this world have been. They have drunk the devil's Kool-Aid and believe his lies concerning the character and nature of God, the person of Jesus, the cross, the empty tomb, the way of genuine salvation, and the reality of hell. Tragically, when it comes to God's truth versus the devil's lies, the vast majority side with Satan. Why is that?

What is it that makes the devil's lies so believable? I think it has to do with the fact that his lies are subtle, clever, reasonable, and appealing to the sinful desires of our flesh. But make no mistake, all his lies are like a baited hook to an unsuspecting, hungry fish. His deceptions promise instant and lasting satisfaction, but they only produce a lifetime of misery that will eventually culminate in an eternity of misery. His falsehoods are not without purpose. Jesus told us the thief has come only "to steal, and kill, and destroy" (John 10:10). I think we would all agree that the devil has accomplished much on his "to do" list of destruction.

Do you remember the 1984 movie classic, *The Terminator*? It was an epic role for Arnold Schwarzenegger. In the iconic sci-fi film, Arnold plays a relentless cyborg assassin who is depicted as an unstoppable force, single-mindedly pursuing his target, Sarah Connor, with cold, mechanical precision. The Terminator has no regard for compassion, mercy, or reason. He comes to kill and destroy—period, end of story!

I believe that the devil, the enemy of our souls, is the original Terminator. He wants to destroy your life and mine. He wants to bring death to purity, faith, hope, and love.

Unlike the Terminator in the movie, the devil is not openly hunting you down with a shotgun in broad daylight. Oh, no. He is far too cunning for that public tactic. Instead, he works through crafty lies and deceitful schemes, trying to get you to believe that God is not good, not truthful, and not worthy of your trust. The only effective way to combat his lies is to expose them to the truth of the Word of God!

The chapters before you in this book, *The Devil's Newsroom,* have been designed to drag the darkness of the devil's biggest lies into the light of God's all-powerful truth. When Satan's lies, as plausible as they often seem, are confronted with the truth, and his dark deceptions meet the light of the Lord, the light and the truth will always prevail. As we honestly evaluate our spiritual beliefs against the revealed Word of God, we discover that we can trust God and His word in any and every situation. As Hebrews 6:18 clearly tells us, "it is impossible for God to lie."

I hope the topics and the Bible passages shared in this book will cause you to see things more clearly than ever. May the devil's fake news be exposed so that you may be grounded in the rock-solid truth of God. My prayer is that this work would bless, encourage, and motivate you to walk in the light with Jesus Christ, the King of kings and Lord of lords.

—DR. JEFF SCHREVE
Pastor
Texarkana, Texas

-1-

The Fake Newscaster

Fake news.

It's a term we hear tossed around quite a bit these days.

People on the right side of the political fence don't like what the left-leaning media has to say and call it "fake." At the same time, people on the left side of the fence make the same objection about right-leaning media. It doesn't always make for inspiring television. In fact, it can sound more like an elementary school playground.

"You're FAKE!"

"No! YOU'RE fake!"

"Am not!"

"Are too!"

In the bygone days of Walter Cronkite, Peter Jennings, and David Brinkley, previous generations just assumed the news was news. But these days, we find ourselves saying, "Is this really true? I don't know if I believe this stuff at all!"

Someone once defined fake news as "journalistic propaganda consisting of deliberate misinformation spread in print, broadcast, or social

> *We can actually identify, with complete assurance, the very first practitioner of fake news. He is none other than the devil himself.*

media with the intent to mislead in order to gain financially, politically, or in some other way."

The truth is that fake news isn't really a modern phenomenon at all. It's much, much older than Twitter, cable news, and Facebook. In the 1930s, when Hitler rose to power, fake news was all over Germany. In that day and age, people really didn't have a way to fact-check what they were hearing about their country and the world. Was what they kept saying on German radio true, or were they all government lies?

But fake news didn't start with Nazi Germany. It goes all the way back to the early days of creation.

And it all starts with a fake newscaster.

Where Fake News Begins

We can actually identify, with complete assurance, the very first practitioner of fake news. He is none other than the devil himself.

Jesus made this clear in the gospel of John, chapter 8. The Lord had been arguing with the religious leaders of His day. They were coming after Him with verbal guns blazing. It was getting just a little heated, to put it mildly.

At one point, the leaders tried to make it sharply personal, throwing these words in the Lord's face: "They said to Him, 'We were not born of fornication; we have one Father, even God.'" Actually, the comment had much more of a vicious edge to it. In the Message paraphrase, they angrily replied to Him, "We're not bastards. We have a legitimate father: the one and only God."

Of course, this was a deliberate slam. Word had no doubt spread that Jesus was the son of Mary—a young woman who was pregnant (by the Holy Spirit) before she married her husband, Joseph. (The people of the first century were not fools. They could do simple math and count to nine. And they balked at the idea that she was with child by the Holy Spirit).

Jesus ignored that pointed barb of illegitimacy and astutely answered with these words:

> "You are of your father the devil, and you want to do the desires of your father. He was a murderer from the beginning, and does not stand in the truth because there is no truth in him. Whenever he speaks a lie, he speaks from his own nature, *for he is a liar and the father of lies."*
>
> —John 8:44, emphasis mine

There it is! The headwaters of deceit and untruth. Every lie that has ever been told can be traced back to the original liar, the OG of liars, and the father of falsehoods. Fake news began with the devil, and he still broadcasts it 24/7 on every channel in every city, however, and wherever he can find an audience.

Why does he do it? It's no big mystery. Satan spreads fake news in order to deceive you and me—and everyone else in the world. But it's not just deception for deception's sake. Those lies *lead* somewhere. If you get taken in by the lies of the devil and choose to follow where they lead, you will ultimately follow them all the way to an eternal hell.

Satan isn't in the fake news business for financial gain. And he couldn't care less about politics; he will use any party, label, or ideology for his own ends. He can be a staunch conservative one moment and a flaming progressive the next. He has had one purpose since being ejected from heaven: to warp and, if possible, destroy the plan of God. That includes wanting to warp and destroy your life and mine.

Why would he do this? What's his motivation? Is there a backstory here? In fact, there is.

The Backstory

As we read the creation story in Genesis, we're almost startled by the sudden and unannounced appearance of a mysterious being. A perfect man and a perfect woman were seemingly getting acquainted with their perfect surroundings in the Garden of Eden when someone else entered the scene.

> "Now the serpent was more crafty than any beast of the field which the Lord God had made. And he said to the woman, "Indeed, has God said, 'You shall not eat from any tree of the garden'?"
>
> —Genesis 3:1

Where did this "serpent" come from, questioning God and twisting His Word? The Bible doesn't tell us in the book of Genesis, but we do gain key insights into his origins from the prophetic book of Ezekiel.

Quickly summarizing here, the Lord had told His prophet Ezekiel to go and speak to a particular world ruler, the king of Tyre.[1] This ancient king of Tyre was an evil ruler named Ethbaal III (591-572 BC). Ezekiel 28 expresses a divine word of judgment and retribution against this wicked king.[2]

---

[1] Footnote: [1]Tyre still exists to this day in modern-day Lebanon—a city of 117,000 people north of Israel on the coast of the Mediterranean Sea. Tyre reigned from 591-573 BC

[2] Footnote: John Walvoord and Roy Zuck, eds. The Bible Knowledge Commentary Old Testament: An Exposition of the Scriptures, 7th Edition (Victor Books, 1989), p. 1282

But something startling happens around verse 11.

God seems to shift gears from the earthly king of Tyre to a being far more privileged and preeminent. Many Bible scholars believe verses 11-19 of Ezekiel 28 speak cryptically of the one known as Satan. He was the real power, the invisible power behind the throne of Tyre. It's worth taking time to read the next nine verses—mysterious as they are—very carefully.

"Again the word of the LORD came to me, saying,
"Son of man, take up a lamentation over the king of Tyre and say to him,
'Thus says the LORD God,
"You had the seal of perfection,
Full of wisdom and perfect in beauty.
You were in Eden, the garden of God;
Every precious stone was your covering:
The ruby, the topaz and the diamond;
The beryl, the onyx and the jasper;
The lapis lazuli, the turquoise and the emerald;
And the gold, the workmanship of your settings and sockets,
Was in you.
On the day that you were created
They were prepared.
You were the anointed cherub who covers,
And I placed you there.
You were on the holy mountain of God;
You walked in the midst of the stones of fire.
You were blameless in your ways
From the day you were created
Until unrighteousness was found in you.
By the abundance of your trade
You were internally filled with violence,
And you sinned;
Therefore I have cast you as profane

From the mountain of God.
And I have destroyed you, O covering cherub,
From the midst of the stones of fire.
Your heart was lifted up because of your beauty;
You corrupted your wisdom by reason of your splendor.
I cast you to the ground;
I put you before kings,
That they may see you.
By the multitude of your iniquities,
In the unrighteousness of your trade
You profaned your sanctuaries.
Therefore I have brought fire from the midst of you;
It has consumed you,
And I have turned you to ashes on the earth
In the eyes of all who see you.
All who know you among the peoples
Are appalled at you;
You have become terrified
And you will cease to be forever.""”

—Ezekiel 28:11-19

This passage gives us a snapshot—or at least a glimpse—of how the devil came to be who he is. In the next few pages, I want to note three discoveries from these verses that give us insight into our adversary's backstory. It's the very fountainhead of fake news in our world today. Note: I was first introduced to this important teaching concerning Satan's origins in a sermon by my hero and mentor from afar, the late, great, Dr. Adrian Rogers. I credit him with opening my eyes to these astonishing findings tucked away in Ezekiel 28.[3]

---

[3] Footnote : Adrian Rogers. "Unmasking Satan's Lies (1746)." Love Worth Finding Ministries, December 10, 2018. Last accessed October, 2024 https://www.lwf.org/sermons/audio/unmasking-satans-lies-1746.

First Discovery: Satan was Originally *Created* by God as a Holy Angel

People often ask, "Why would God create a being as evil as the devil?" But God didn't create the devil. *He created a perfect, radiant, stunningly beautiful angel.*

The devil's original name was Lucifer, or "light-bearer." He was also called "star of the morning" and "son of the dawn" (Isaiah 14:12). In Ezekiel 28:12, God says to him, "You had the seal of perfection, full of wisdom and perfect in beauty." There was no blemish, defect, or sin in this mighty celestial being—not even a shadow of a shadow. In verse 15, the Lord declares to him, "You were blameless in your ways from the day you were created."

And he wasn't only a *perfect* angel; he was a preeminent angel—the masterpiece of an angelic world so vast, multi-layered, and glorious that we can't begin to wrap our minds around it. These few words in the Book of Ezekiel are like a quick peek through the curtain into a higher universe far beyond our own.

Ezekiel 28:14 says, "You were the anointed cherub who covers." What's a cherub? Well, it's most certainly *not* an obese baby angel with a bow and arrow. (Cupid certainly doesn't cut the mustard here.) In reality, a cherub is the highest of the angelic order—an awesome, glorious, powerful spirit being.

When God instructed Moses about how to build the ark of the covenant, the iconic symbol of God's presence in the Old Testament, He specified that two cherubim would be on the top of the lid. Formed of solid gold, their wings were to overshadow the ark, touching in the middle.

The NIV translation of Ezekiel 28:14 reads, "You were anointed as a guardian cherub, for so I ordained you." Do you know who Lucifer once was? Drum roll, please, to prepare us for this shocking news: he was once the guardian angel of God! What a supreme honor! What greater privilege

> *The Creator was never created. He has no*
>
> *beginning, and He will have no end.*

and responsibility could any being have in the whole universe? Lucifer was the anointed cherub who guarded God.

The book of Ezekiel goes on to speak about the covering of this preeminent angel. It specifically mentions precious stones: ruby, topaz, diamond, beryl, onyx, jasper, sapphire, turquoise, and emerald. All of those stones were in the breastpiece of the high priest, as recorded in the book of Exodus, chapter 29. Without getting too carried away here, we might even think of him as the prime minister of heaven.

In Ezekiel 28:13, Scripture mentions "the gold, the workmanship of your settings and sockets." That's one way of reading it. But it's interesting to note that the word for *settings* could also mean "tambourines," and the word for *sockets* could mean "pipes." Some have speculated that there was a musical quality inherent in Lucifer's nature. Perhaps Lucifer was the worship leader of heaven. One can only speculate. But the oft-told joke that when the devil fell, he landed in the choir loft is not without some scriptural connection.

Just imagine this beautiful, exalted cherub leading myriads of angels across the heavens in worship to the Lord. What do you think it would have looked like if God's blazing *shekinah* (meaning: Gods presence) glory shone through those precious stones of the "anointed cherub who covers"?

Earthly eyes can't envision such things, and physical imaginations can't begin to process the unfathomable splendor. But Ezekiel 28 describes something incredibly powerful and vastly beautiful for a clear purpose: God wants us to understand the extreme heights from which Lucifer fell.

The Lord said,

"By the abundance of your trade You were internally filled with violence, And you sinned; Therefore I have cast you as profane From the mountain of God. And I have destroyed you, O covering cherub, From the midst of the stones of fire."

—Ezekiel 28:16

All of heaven must have watched that terrible fall. Even Jesus presumably alluded to this scene when He told His disciples, "I was watching Satan fall from heaven like lightning" (Luke 10:18).

Now there is one incredibly important word repeated in Ezekiel 28 verses 13 and 15 that we dare not overlook.

It is the word *CREATED*.

Scripture says of the Lord, "Before the mountains were born Or You gave birth to the earth and the world, Even from everlasting to everlasting, You are God" (Psalm 90:2). In other words, the Creator was never created. He has no beginning, and He will have no end. He is "the Alpha and Omega, the first and the last, the beginning and the end" (Revelation 22:13). And no, I can't comprehend that either. It blows my mind to consider the eternality of God. But I believe it because the Bible teaches this truth over and over again.

Satan, however, is a created being—created as Lucifer, the chief of the angelic beings. God Himself gave him life and privileged him with an exalted position. Lucifer was the most powerful of angels, but he was never all-powerful. Omnipotence is reserved for God alone. Make no mistake; the Creator has more power in His little finger than Lucifer/Satan does in his whole being.

Second Discovery: Satan was Corrupted by Sin

Not only was Lucifer/Satan created by God, but he was also corrupted by sin.

Ezekiel 28:15-16 tells us: "You were blameless in your ways from the day you were created until unrighteousness was found in you. By the abundance of your trade, you were internally filled with violence and you sinned; Therefore, I have cast you as profane from the mountain of God. And I have destroyed you, O covering cherub, from the midst of the stones of fire."

He was with God on the mountain of God, which speaks of God's government and kingdom. He was God's guardian angel, as close to Him as you can get. As previously mentioned, it is quite possible that he led the vast host of angels in worship. No created being could match him for sheer intelligence, magnificence, and splendor.

But then he sinned and fell, hard and far.

The Scripture says unrighteousness was found in him. Where would that have come from? How could there be any seeds of unrighteousness in a perfect, sinless heaven? Theologians have been discussing and debating that question for centuries. Surely, we will not know the answer on this side of heaven. But what we can deduce from Scripture is the nature of Satan's original sin. I believe it was three-fold transgression.

Transgression #1: Pride

In another Old Testament passage, we get a second brief glimpse of what happened when Lucifer fell. The book of Isaiah gives us this picture in Isaiah 14:12-14. I like how this passage reads in the New King James Version:

> "How you are fallen from heaven,
> O Lucifer, son of the morning!
> *How* you are cut down to the ground,
> You who weakened the nations!
> For you have said in your heart:
> 'I will ascend into heaven,
> I will exalt my throne above the stars of God;
> I will also sit on the mount of the congregation
> On the farthest sides of the north;
> I will ascend above the heights of the clouds,
> I will be like the Most High."

Let that last line sink in—*"I will be like the Most High."* The New American Standard records it this way: "I will make myself like the Most High." Lucifer's lofty declaration simply oozes with rotten pride.

It's good to remember that the middle letter in the word "pride" is "I." It's the same letter in the word "sin." Pride and sin are "I" problems. Let's be honest here and admit that we've seen it in ourselves, just as we have seen it in others. But it all began with Satan. He had an "I" problem. Five times in the passage above, he said two little words: *"I will."* We have to conclude that he just couldn't handle the lofty position of honor he had been given. Maybe he started thinking something like this: "All of this praise that is going *through* me needs to come *to* me. I know what I will do. I will raise my throne above God's, and I will make myself like the Most High."

But God's response to Lucifer's five-fold "I will" was a resounding "No, you will not!" In Isaiah 14:15 (ESV), God says, "you will be thrust down to Sheol, to the recesses of the pit." And Lucifer, the star of the morning, the son of the dawn, became Satan, the father of the night and all that is evil.

Pride was Satan's first sin—and no doubt the first sin ever committed in all creation. When it comes to sin, any sin, pride is always involved. It is pride that says, "I will do what I want to do."

Solomon hit the nail on the head when he wrote: "Pride goes before destruction, And a haughty spirit before stumbling" (Proverbs 16:18). It was true for Lucifer, and it's true for each one of us. When pride comes on the scene, get ready for a fall.

But there was another sin that occurred right alongside the sin of pride.

Transgression #2: Ingratitude

What's the ingratitude here? Just think about what God had given him! Just consider the mind-boggling position of honor and privilege with which he had been entrusted. He was the number one angel God had

Pride was Satan's first sin—and no doubt the first sin ever committed in all creation. When it comes to sin, any sin, pride is always involved.

made. Out of all the countless heavenly beings, he got the top spot. But instead of being grateful, even humbled at such an honor, he thought he should have even *more* power and glory and authority.

I can imagine him saying to himself, "Why should there be someone above me? Look how beautiful I am. Look at the wisdom I possess. Look at the sound that comes from me, the music that echoes from me throughout the halls of heaven. Why am I not sitting on the throne?" He was ungrateful for what God had given him. He wasn't satisfied with being the prime minister of heaven. He wanted the crown. So, he allowed his pride and ingratitude to produce a third deadly strand of sin.

Transgression #3: Rebellion

Pride . . . ingratitude . . . and rebellion. That was Satan's threefold sin that led to his fall from the heights of heaven.

In Revelation 12:3-4a we encounter another name for fallen Lucifer: *the dragon.*

> "Then another sign appeared in heaven: and behold, a great red dragon having seven heads and ten horns, and on his heads were seven diadems. And his tail swept away a third of the stars of heaven and threw them to the earth."

> Revelation 20:2 refers to him as "the serpent of old, who is the devil and Satan . . . ."

What does the Bible mean when it says that this dragon's tail swept a third of the stars from heaven and cast them down to the earth?

Many Bible scholars believe that Lucifer, who had authority over all the untold myriads of angels, somehow enticed a third of them to join him in his rebellion against God. These "fallen angels" became what we know today as demons or evil spirits. They join with Satan to fight against the good plan and purposes of God. How many demons are there? The Bible doesn't give us a number. We do know, however, that God's holy angels outnumber the demons two to one. Now think with me for a moment about this threefold sin of Satan: pride, ingratitude, and rebellion. Those three sins are the footprints of the devil, this fallen creature. And because we too are fallen beings, we make these same footprints on our own.

What About Us?

In our *pride,* we say, "It's my life, and I will do what I want to do. I'm the captain of my own ship. If I want to drink, I'll drink. If I want to do drugs, I'll do drugs. If I want to lie, cheat, steal, or engage in sexual immorality, I'm going to do it. If I want to carry bitterness in my heart toward someone who did me wrong, that's my business. I have every right to hate and exact revenge on those who hurt me." Can you see the pride and the self-centeredness involved in sin?

There's also *ingratitude.* We become dissatisfied with what we have and what God has given us. We're like the Israelites in the wilderness, who felt wonder and awe when God rained down manna—the bread of angels—on their camp every morning. It was good to taste, easy to gather, and completely nutritious. But it didn't take too many manna meals before they couldn't stop complaining about it: "We remember the fish which we used to eat free in Egypt, the cucumbers and the melons and the leeks and the onions and the garlic, but now our appetite is gone. There is nothing at all to look at except this manna" (Numbers 11:5-6). Instead of being grateful, they were hateful.

We often talk ourselves into thinking life is unfair, that we always get the short end of the stick, and God really doesn't care about us. When thoughts like these begin working in our hearts, what happens next? *Rebellion.* We find ourselves in danger of turning our backs on the Word of God, the will of God, and the ways of God.

When you think about it, Satan used the same threefold approach against Eve in the Garden of Eden. He worked on her in the realms of pride, ingratitude, and rebellion. For some incomprehensible reason, she believed the lie that God was "holding out" on her and she wasn't getting her just due. She may have told herself, "If I could just eat a little of that beautiful, forbidden fruit, I could become like God. I would know good and evil and wouldn't need to depend on God so much." Eve brazenly fell from her state of innocence through pride, ingratitude, and rebellion—and she persuaded her husband, Adam, to eat (and fall) with her.

Third Discovery: Satan Continues to Exist for a Divine Purpose

If God created the devil, why doesn't He just eradicate him forever? Why doesn't He remove him from the scene? Without question, the One who spoke him into existence could easily speak him into oblivion. So, why doesn't He? We certainly would if we were God.

Needless to say, that is a very hard question to definitively answer. The Lord tells us in Isaiah 55:8, "'For My thoughts are not your thoughts, nor are your ways My ways,' declares the LORD." While we cannot always know why God does what He does, we can know that God is perfect in all He does. We can always trust His ways, even when they don't make sense to us.

When God saw what had happened with Lucifer, He heard him say in his heart, "I will, I will, I will, I will, I will," and then the LORD replied with an "I will" of His own. In effect, God responded, "You say that you will ascend, Lucifer? Well, I will descend and become a man. I will defeat you forever—not as God, squashing you like a bug on the sidewalk, but as a man who is depending on God." And that's exactly what He did.

It's important to remember that when the Lord created Adam and Eve, He gave this first couple *dominion* over the whole earth (Genesis 1:28). In Genesis chapter 2, Adam exercised that dominion, naming all the beasts and birds in the world.

But in Genesis chapter 3, dominion was lost. When Adam and Eve sinned, something died inside of them, and they lost their dominion over the earth and its creatures. Furthermore, they became the slaves of sin and Satan. Their God-given dominion was legally forfeited when they deliberately disobeyed the Lord.

Was it lost forever? How could that dominion ever come back?

Here's how.

It comes back when God Himself becomes a man and defeats the devil— not as God, but as a man, depending upon God.

The Second Adam

In the book of 1 Corinthians, we read about "the second Adam."

> So also it is written, "The first MAN, Adam, BECAME A LIVING SOUL." The last Adam *became* a life-giving spirit. However, the spiritual is not first, but the natural; then the spiritual. The first man is from the earth, earthy; the second man is from heaven. As is the earthy, so also are those who are earthy; and as is the heavenly, so also are those who are heavenly. Just as we have borne the image of the earthy, we will also bear the image of the heavenly."
>
> —1 Corinthians 15:45-49

Who's the last Adam, the second Adam? It's the Lord Jesus Christ. You see, from God's viewpoint, only two men ever lived: Adam and Christ. The Bible says, "For as in Adam all die, so also in Christ all will be

While we cannot always know why God does what He does, we can know that God is perfect in all He does. We can always trust His ways, even when they don't make sense to us.

Pastor Jeff

made alive" (1 Corinthians 15:22). When you are born into this world, you are born in Adam. What happens to all those "in Adam"? They all die! There is no escape and no hope. The world is enslaved to sin and Satan, and the children of Adam are destined for eternal death. But Jesus left His throne in heaven, put on human flesh, and defeated the devil at the cross. As a result, the dominion that Adam legally lost was legally regained by the Lord Jesus. And man born in Adam could become man born-again in Christ—and live!

When Jesus was dying on the cross, you may remember one of the last things He said: *"It is finished!"* (John 19:30)

He didn't say, "I am finished," but rather, "IT is finished." The word He used—*tetelestai*—means "paid in full"! It was a marketplace word written on business transactions whenever payment was fully received. As Jesus breathed His last on the cross, He cried out, *"Tetelestai!"* Did Satan understand the implications of that utterance? Maybe he was in the dark until the third day—when Christ arose!

On that third day, did the enemy say to himself, "He came out of the grave . . . and now I am finished!"?

The Bible tells us that when Jesus rose from the dead, He had "the keys of death and of Hades" (Revelation 1:18). The devil had lost his keys and his dominion. Jesus Christ defeated him through the cross and the empty tomb.

Listen to these great words from the book of Hebrews: "Therefore, since the children share in flesh and blood, He Himself likewise also partook of the same, *that through death He might render powerless him who had the power of death, that is, the devil.*" (Hebrews 2:14, emphasis mine)

God defeated the devil through the second Adam, the man Christ Jesus. The devil said, "I will, I will, I will, I will, I will." And Jesus said, "Not My will, but Yours [Father] be done." What a massive contrast between Satan and the Son of God.

Satan Continues

Yes, Satan continues on to this day. He continues to do his utmost to block men and women from learning the truth about salvation in Christ. He works overtime to keep people in spiritual darkness and enslaved to sin.

But his plans for ultimate conquest have been shredded, and he knows his time is short. His back has been broken. As Adrian Rogers liked to say, "He sails a sinking ship and rules a doomed domain."[4]

Why doesn't the Lord just obliterate him—right now? He will send him to hell forever one day, but that day hasn't arrived yet. In the meantime, we know God uses the devil as an object lesson.

Back in Ezekiel 28:17, the Lord said to Satan:

"Your heart was lifted up because of your beauty;
You corrupted your wisdom by reason of your splendor.
I cast you to the ground;
I put you before kings,
That they may see you."

In essence, God seems to be saying, "I want to keep you around so that the kings of earth will see you, broken and defeated."

In the Old Testament, when one army would defeat another, the victorious army would often take the king of that defeated country and parade him in chains behind their chariots. Everybody would laugh at that vanquished king and mock the one who was now so powerless. That is a picture of what God is going to do with Satan. God is going to use Satan as an object lesson to say before the universe, "Behold, the creature who was proud, ungrateful, and rebellious. He thought he could take Me on. Just look at him now."

---

[4] Footnote: Daily Devotional: Who Or What Are You... (2021) Love Worth Finding Ministries. Accessed 14 August 2024. URL.

All will see the once prideful and powerful devil totally humiliated, completely debased, and utterly destroyed. Ezekiel 28:19 says, "All who know you among the peoples are appalled at you; You have become terrified and you will cease to be forever." A day is coming at the end of time as we know it, when God will cast the devil into the lake of fire—and he will be tormented forever and ever.

But in the meantime, Satan, the first and foremost fake newscaster, continues to broadcast lies, deceptions, and crooked narratives to mislead, deceive, and destroy every person he possibly can. He isn't a bit particular to which media, publication, or channel he uses. He will use Hollywood, the music industry, TV news, newspapers, social media, magazines, etc. He will even use church pulpits—a favorite of his—whenever he can.

The apostle Paul told the Corinthian Christians he was staying alert and aware, "so that no advantage would be taken of us by Satan, for we are not ignorant of his schemes." (2 Corinthians 2:11)

In a world swamped by the devil's fake news, Paul's plan sounds like a *great* plan.

-2-

Liar, Liar

Every year, the little village of Santon Bridge in northwest England holds a unique and widely celebrated competition—and it isn't an athletic contest, a spelling bee, or a cribbage tournament.

In mid-November, contestants from around the world gather at a little pub, The Bridge Inn, to determine who rates as the World's Biggest Liar. A carefully selected panel of judges gives each fib-teller five minutes to spin the biggest and most convincing whopper they can come up with. Competition rules bar the use of props, scripts, or notes.

One man has won the dubious honor seven times—the most outrageous liar for seven years running. Anyone can enter the contest, with one stipulation: you can't be a politician because then, they say, you would be a *pro*, and this is strictly an amateur's competition.

Each year someone walks away from Santon Bridge with the World's Biggest Liar trophy tucked under his or her arm. But we know better, don't we? These are only bush-league, B-team deceivers. The world's biggest liar doesn't reside in England, America, Canada, or Micronesia.

Satan owns the title of the World's Biggest Liar

because he tells lies about the biggest and most

important subject of all: God Himself.

The world's biggest liar is also the world's original liar—the devil. Jesus said of him, "He was a murderer from the beginning, and does not stand in the truth, because there is no truth in him. When he lies, he speaks out of his own character, for he is a liar and the father of lies" (John 8:44, ESV). The Message paraphrase puts it this way: "He couldn't stand the truth because there wasn't a shred of truth in him. When the Liar speaks, he makes it up out of his lying nature and fills the world with lies."

Satan owns the title of the World's Biggest Liar because he tells lies about the biggest and most important subject of all: God Himself.

The devil is not only the biggest liar, but he is also the best liar. Since the dawn of civilization, myriads of people have believed his lies and readily swallowed his deception hook, line, and sinker. The Scripture says of the devil that he is "the deceiver of the whole world" (Revelation 12:9). He is the most abominable liar because his lies, if you believe them, will wreck and ruin your life and send you to hell forever.

In this chapter, we will examine Genesis 3 and the devil's first encounter with our original parents, Adam and Eve. Scripture, of course, is true from cover to cover. But Genesis 3 is critical to every one of us because it is foundational to everything else that follows, from Genesis 4 right through the last chapter of Revelation.

Perhaps this is why Genesis 3 has come under such sustained attack throughout the years. Critics and opponents have labeled this all-important biblical account as a "fable" or "Jewish myth." But here's the truth: You can't understand the gospel and you can't comprehend the life and ministry of Jesus

Christ unless and until you grapple with the third chapter of Genesis. If Genesis 3 is a myth, then John 3 is ridiculous. In John 3:7, Jesus said, "You must be born again." But if there is no fall of man, there is no need to be reborn.

Genesis 3:1-9 is certainly true, and here is what it says:

"Now the serpent was more crafty than any beast of the field which the LORD God had made. And he said to the woman, "Has God really said, 'You shall not eat from any tree of the garden'?" The woman said to the serpent, "From the fruit of the trees of the garden we may eat; but from the fruit of the tree which is in the middle of the garden, God has said, 'You shall not eat from it or touch it, or you will die.'" The serpent said to the woman, "You certainly will not die! For God knows that on the day you eat from it your eyes will be opened, and you will become like God, knowing good and evil." When the woman saw that the tree was good for food, and that it was a delight to the eyes, and that the tree was desirable to make *one* wise, she took some of its fruit and ate; and she also gave *some* to her husband with her, and he ate. Then the eyes of both of them were opened, and they knew that they were naked; and they sewed fig leaves together and made themselves waist coverings. Now they heard the sound of the LORD God walking in the garden in the cool of the day, and the man and his wife hid themselves from the presence of the LORD God among the trees of the garden. Then the LORD God called to the man, and said to him, "Where are you?"

Notice with me three discoveries about the devil's lies. Not all of his lies are the same kind.

First Discovery: The Devil Speaks *Subtle* Lies

The J. B. Phillips translation of Genesis 3:1 says that "the serpent was clever, more clever than any wild animal God had made."

Don't look for the devil to appear in a red suit

with horns, hooves, and a pitchfork. The evil one

is much more subtle and clever than that.

When we read this, we naturally equate this serpent with Satan. But did he actually come slithering through the grass up to Eve in the Garden of Eden as a snake? I tend to think he didn't. It wasn't until after they ate from the tree and hid from God that God cursed the "serpent" to crawl on his belly: "Cursed are you above all livestock and all wild animals! You will crawl on your belly and you will eat dust all the days of your life" (Genesis 3:14, NIV). Based on this passage, I don't imagine that Eve found herself looking down at a rattlesnake with a forked tongue or the twisting coils of a massive python.

Bible commentator Ray Stedman points out that the Hebrew word translated *serpent* in this passage comes from a root that means "the shining one" or "to shine." As we noted in the previous chapter, Satan wasn't created as the prime minister of evil. He was created as Lucifer, "O star of the morning, son of the dawn" (Isaiah 14:12). He was the shining one, "the anointed cherub who covers" (Ezekiel 28:14). He *became* the devil through his own rebellious actions.

In 2 Corinthians 11:14, the Apostle Paul tells us, "Satan disguises himself as an angel of light." In other words, the devil knows how to dress like one of God's holy angels, even though he is dark and evil to the core. He adorns himself with a mask of light and beauty, but it is only a surface disguise.

Did he come to Eve as a shining, attractive creature, approaching her through the trees in a halo of light, or as a hideous serpent? The former seems to be more in line with the warning Paul gave of him and his masquerade of radiance. Therefore, don't look for the devil to appear in a red suit with horns, hooves, and a pitchfork. The evil one is much more subtle and clever than that.

Regardless of how Satan may have presented himself, we can know that he slithered quietly into the Garden of Eden, unannounced and perhaps undetected. Apparently, Eve was not in the least bit startled, frightened, or sickened by the appearance of this serpent. She doesn't shrink away from him and, in her innocence, doesn't seem at all surprised that this creature would approach her and speak to her. (Skeptics love to mock believers, sarcastically asking if we believe in talking snakes. I always answer, "I believe in a talking devil.")

How does the serpent begin the conversation? It all starts with one little question.

> "Indeed has God said, 'You shall not eat from any tree of the garden?"
>
> —Genesis 3:1

The serpent's question is loaded with deadly poison—but it is a subtle poison. He says, in effect, "Hey, Eve. I'm just trying to understand something here, and maybe you can help me out. Has God really said that you can't eat from any tree in the garden? Boy, that just doesn't sound right, does it? Is that what He really said?"

Actually, that is *not* what God had said. What God said to Adam was this: "From any tree of the garden you may eat freely; but from the tree of the knowledge of good and evil you shall not eat, for in the day you eat from it you shall surely die" (Genesis 2:16-17).

Do you see how subtle and crafty the devil is here? He takes God's word and immediately and deliberately twists and distorts it. In his opening line to Eve, he slyly questions both the word of God and the character and goodness of God. Let me paraphrase his meaning: "Eve, has God really said you can't eat from any tree in the garden? Seriously? That makes absolutely no

The moment you start to question whether the Bible is true and whether the things God says in the Bible are true, you are walking into Satan's trap, just as Eve did.

sense! Why would He create all these beautiful fruit trees laden with fruit and then forbid you to eat them? That doesn't ring true at all. And if He really said you can't eat of any tree . . . oh my goodness . . . what does that say about His character? What a sadistic, malevolent deity He must be."

Right off the bat, he tries to get Eve to question God's Word and to doubt His goodness and character. And let's not kid ourselves; the evil one works the same way in your life and mine. Do you ever question some parts of Scripture—maybe having doubts about what you're reading? When you read the Bible and come across something you don't really like or understand, do you begin to question? "Well, that must just be a cultural thing. That doesn't make sense in today's world, so I'm going to set that part of the Word aside."

Some people think of the Bible like a cafeteria, where you slide your tray down the line and select a little bit of this, a little bit of that, and say "No, thank you," to the dishes that don't appeal to you. Be very careful about that approach! The moment you start to question whether the Bible is true and whether the things God says in the Bible are true, you are walking into Satan's trap, just as Eve did.

Even Billy Graham, early in his ministry, experienced attacks of doubt about the reliability of God's Word. Back in the late 1940s, he had a contemporary preacher friend named Charles Templeton. Charles was a gifted communicator, but he was wavering in his faith. He told Billy something like this: "Listen! I've been to seminary, and there are so many questions about the Bible that nobody can answer. Obviously, this book is old and archaic and doesn't stand up to the test of time. You can't rely on what you read in those pages. You can't believe Genesis 3 and, really, the first eleven chapters of Genesis. It's just all a story. A myth. Noah didn't really exist. There wasn't an ark."

He kept filling Billy Graham's ears with all the stuff that, quite frankly, people keep repeating to this day. "God didn't create the world by the power of His Word as it says in Genesis. The creation account was never meant to be taken literally. Obviously, it all took place over billions and billions of years of evolution." As a young man, Billy Graham was really struggling in the face of Templeton's attacks because he couldn't answer his questions. His friend would press him, saying, "Billy, how can this be?" And Graham would just shake his head and say, "I don't know."

Late one night in the foothills of San Bernadino, California, Graham went out into the woods alone with his Bible. Setting his open Bible on a stump, he got down on his knees and prayed this prayer: "O God! There are many things in this book I do not understand. There are many problems with it for which I have no solution. There are many seeming contradictions. There are some areas in it that do not seem to correlate with modern science. I can't answer some of the philosophical and psychological questions Chuck and others are raising. Father, I am going to accept this as thy word—by faith! I am going to allow faith to go beyond my intellectual questions and doubts, and I will believe this to be Your inspired Word!"

In later years, when Graham was relating this story, he said that the moment he made that decision, a deep peace flooded his heart. And from that time on, his preaching had power like never before. Soon after that prayer in the woods, Billy Graham preached at the 1949 Los Angeles Crusade. It was supposed to last for three weeks, but it went on for *eight* weeks. Over 350,000 people came to hear Billy Graham preach in those eight weeks, and 3,000 people made commitments to follow Jesus Christ.[1]

---

[1] Footnote: Will Graham. "The Tree Stump Prayer: When Billy Graham Overcame Doubt." Billy Graham Evangelistic Association. 2014. https://billygraham.org/story/the-tree-stump-prayer-where-billy-graham-overcame-doubt/.

Louis Zamperini, whose life story *Unbroken* became a bestselling book and a major movie, received Christ at that crusade. So did Stuart Hamblen, who became known as "the singing cowboy" and a major recording artist in his day. How did Billy Graham get catapulted into a worldwide ministry? It may very well have started when he got down on his knees in the woods with an open Bible before him and said, "God, this is Your Word, and I'm going to believe it, even if I don't understand all of it."

One of Satan's chief goals with Eve in the Garden of Eden was to create doubt in her innocent heart and cause her to question the goodness and character of her God.

Sometimes, all the evil one seeks to do is plant a tiny seed of doubt. "Can I trust God? Is He really good? If God made all these trees and says that I can't eat from them, then, well, maybe He's holding out on me. Maybe He's not as good as I thought He was."

Please take these next words to heart. Every Christian—man or woman, young or old—needs to have these two truths chiseled in his or her heart: *God is good,* and *God loves me.* Why is this so critical? Because if you don't maintain a firm grip on these twin truths, you won't be able to stand strong when you're slammed with a storm of heartaches and trials. When the circumstances of life kick you in the teeth and punch you in the gut (and they will), you may very well be thrown off course. If you don't know-that-you-know-that-you- know-that-you-know that God is good and that He loves you, you may find yourself slipping from the faith. You may begin to wonder: *Is God really good, or is He mean and cruel? Is God a God who likes to watch me squirm like a worm in hot ashes? Is God a God who allows these terrible things to come into my life and somehow get some sadistic glee from it?*

The Bible leaves no room for doubt. Scripture echoes with words like these:

- "O Give thanks to the LORD, for he is good; For His loving kindness is everlasting." (1 Chronicles 16:34)

- "I will sing to the LORD, because He has dealt bountifully with me." (Psalm 13:6)

- "For you, LORD, are good and ready to forgive, and abundant in loving kindness to all who call upon You." (Psalm 86:5)

- "Oh, taste and see that the LORD is good; how blessed is the man who takes refuge in Him!" (Psalm 34:8)

- "For the LORD God is a sun and shield; the LORD gives grace and glory; No good thing does he withhold from those who walk uprightly." (Psalm 84:11)

In 1 Timothy 6:17, the apostle Paul tells us that God is the One "who richly supplies us with all things to enjoy." God is a good God. But in the very first lie ever told on earth, we witness the serpent questioning that goodness with all the subtlety and craft he could employ.

Second Discovery: Satan Speaks *Blatant* Lies

Going back to that world-changing conversation in the Garden of Eden, the serpent asked,

"…has God said, 'You shall not eat from any tree of the garden'?" The woman said to the serpent, "From the fruit of the trees of the garden we may eat; but from the fruit of the tree which is in the middle of the garden, God has said, 'You shall not eat from it or touch it, or you will die.'"

—Genesis 3:1-3

And the serpent replied, "You surely will not die!"

There was nothing subtle about *that* lie. It was bold and blatant. And Satan keeps using this Big Lie technique to this very day with you and

God is good, and God loves me. Why is this so critical? Because if you don't maintain a firm grip on these twin truths, you won't be able to stand strong when you're slammed with a storm of heartaches and trials.

Pastor Jeff

me. Do you want an example of a blatant lie? Try this one on for size: *You can sin and suffer no consequences. You can sin and get away with it.*

That's one of the biggest falsehoods ever. That's a lie that would put all the liars in Santon Bridge, England, to shame. And the devil is still saying that today. If you have a pen, please underline this: *Sin ALWAYS has consequences—terrible, devastating consequences.*

You can't sin and get away with it.
I can't sin and get away with it.
No one sins and gets away with it.

The devil told our first mother, "Oh, come on, Eve, you're not going to die. That's ridiculous! God may *say* that, but I'm telling you that it's not true." He had already planted doubt in her heart about God's goodness, and now he takes it one huge step further. He says that God can't be trusted. He says that Almighty God, the Creator of the Universe, is a liar.

We hear echoes of that today, from Satan himself and from his huge legion of evil spirits set loose in our world. Sometimes it sounds like this: *You know you want to. Why don't you just do it? Go ahead. It'll be all right. Nobody's going to see. There won't be any consequences—or at least nothing serious. And who's going to know? It's just a little fun, and you won't be addicted. You can just move on like it never happened. Even ask for forgiveness. Whatever.*

The McDonald's slogan from yesteryear said, "You deserve a break today." Not to be outdone, Burger King came up with the catchphrase, "Have it your way." And that's the message from our adversary, the devil. "You need to have your way in this. You deserve this. You don't want to miss out."

But despite what Satan tells us, there really are consequences—and they are devastating. In Numbers 32:23 (NIV) we read, "You may be sure that your sin will find you out." Another translation says, "You can be sure that your sin will track you down." In other words, you can't commit a sin without leaving a forwarding address. And sooner or later, the consequences *will* come knocking on your door.

In the case of Adam and Eve, they knew immediately that something catastrophic had happened. Their lives had changed and could never be the same again. Suddenly, their delightful innocence was gone, and they knew they were naked. Pitifully, they crouched in the bushes and tried to sew fig leaves together to cover themselves up. What *was* that dark, sickening feeling they had never experienced before?

It was shame.

And what was that choking, stomach-churning emotion they sensed when they heard God, their friend, walking in the garden, calling out to them?

It was fear.

Fear? Of their best friend? *Yes.* The Lord had called out, "Where are you?" and Adam answered, "I heard the sound of You in the garden and I was afraid because I was naked, so I hid myself. (Genesis 3:9-10)

Guilt. Shame. Dread. Fear. Humiliation. Despair. All these brand-new emotions came tumbling over Adam and Eve like a black tsunami. Does sin have consequences? Oh, yes. There were consequences higher than the clouds and deeper than the Grand Canyon, and those same dreadful effects would roll through the centuries and millennia until this very day. *Every lie. Every illness. Every tear. Every wound. Every rape. Every murder. Every cruelty. Every misunderstanding. Every war. Every loneliness.*

It all began with that first blatant lie, when the serpent said, "You will not surely die" (Genesis 3:4, NKJV). But God had said, "but from the tree of the knowledge of good and evil you shall not eat, for in the day that you eat from it you will surely die." (Genesis 2:17)

The New Testament book of James tells us that "each person is tempted when they are dragged away by their own evil desire and enticed. Then, after desire has conceived, it gives birth to sin; and sin, when it is full-grown, gives birth to death." (James 1:14-15, NIV)

Pastor Robert Lewis points out that Adam was *with* Eve in this crisis, as she took a bite of that forbidden fruit. What was he doing? Was he watching her to see what happened to her? Did he expect her to drop over dead? And why was he passively standing there while his wife was under attack? Why wasn't he protecting Eve from the velvet-tongued serpent? That's a real mystery. The Apostle Paul points out that Eve had been deceived, but Adam was not deceived. So, why did he also disobey God? That is a mystery to which the Bible does not definitively answer.

Adam certainly didn't drop dead in his tracks after eating the fruit. The biblical record tells us that he lived to be 930 years old (Genesis 5:5). Someone might say, "I guess the serpent was telling the truth when he said they wouldn't die."

But they did die. Both of them. They died immediately inside, in their spirit—that part of their being that communed with the living God. And in that instant, death came into the world. In Romans 5:12(ESV), we read: "Sin came into the world through one man, and death through sin, and so death spread to all men."

A door opened into our beautiful, perfect world that was never meant to be opened and could only be closed at the end of time by God Himself. Just as Satan was the original liar, and every lie that has ever been told springs from him, so death entered the world on the day Adam sinned, and every death through all the ages of our world sprang from that moment.

Sin always brings devastating consequences, but the consequences of sin are often *delayed*. And that's why, as it says in Ecclesiastes 8:11 (NIV), "When the sentence for a crime is not quickly carried out, people's hearts are filled with schemes to do wrong."

People will say, "I cheated on my spouse, but nothing really came of it." Or maybe, "I lied to get my promotion, but no one really noticed." Or possibly, "I lied on my expense reports, but it was no big deal." People will say I did this and that and the other, but nothing has happened to me.

Or has it?

What blessings and wonderful opportunities have you *missed out on* because you deliberately took yourself out of the will of God? The prophet Jonah had it right when he said, "Those who cling to worthless

Sin always brings devastating consequences, but the consequences of sin are often delayed.

idols forfeit the grace that could be theirs" (Jonah 2:8, NIV). What have you and I forfeited because we turned from God's path and went our own way? We may never know.

And speaking of consequences, I'm reminded of the old poem by Henry Wadsworth Longfellow: "Though the mills of God grind slowly, yet they grind exceedingly small; though with patience He stands waiting, with exactness grinds He all."

Consequences follow sin like night follows day. They may not arrive at your doorstep within 24 hours, but they will arrive. In Galatians 6:7-8 (ESV), the Apostle Paul writes:

> "Do not be deceived: God is not mocked, for whatever one sows, that will he also reap. For the one who sows to his own flesh will from the flesh reap corruption, but the one who sows to the Spirit will from the Spirit reap eternal life."

We know about sowing and reaping. We know that if we plant a seed on Friday, we don't reap a crop on Saturday. It takes time. You reap what you sow. You reap more than you sow. You reap later than you sow. And so, when we think, *Hey, I'm getting away with sin,* we're not really escaping consequences at all.

Do you remember the sad story of Achan in the Book of Joshua? The very first Canaanite city the Israelites approached was Jericho, with its high, thick, imposing walls. How intimidating and frightening it must have looked to God's people as they saw those towering walls, bristling with all the state-of-the-art defenses.

Even so, victory was already assured because the Lord had told General Joshua, "See, I have given Jericho into your hand, with its king and mighty men of valor" (Joshua 6:2, ESV). But the Lord had also laid down a very specific rule. All the plunder from the victory, every bit of it, belonged to Him. All the gold and silver and precious articles were to be placed immediately into the Lord's treasury. PERIOD. END OF SENTENCE. The Lord's and Joshua's instructions in that matter couldn't have been clearer.

But there's always one guy who thinks he's the exception to the rule, isn't there? ("Yes, the sign says 65 miles per hour, but that doesn't apply to *me*.")

After the battle, a man named Achan happened to see a beautiful Babylonian cloak (he had never seen anything that snazzy) lying in the ruins—along with a stash of silver and a bar of gold. And he took them for himself. Yes, he remembered what God and Joshua had said, but really, what was the harm? There were tons of this loot, and who would miss this little bit?

He took it back to his tent, and presumably with the knowledge of his whole family, hid the stuff in a hole under his tent.

You can bet that Satan had been there, whispering in this man's ear. Telling him that it wasn't such a big sin after all, that it had been unfair of God to deny the people a few goodies from their victory, and that nobody would ever find out anyway.

A day went by, and nothing happened. Another day, and no one seemed the wiser. Another day and another day and another day and by this time Achan was feeling relieved and telling himself, *Man, I'm home free.* But everything changed after the next battle. Ai was just a little town, and much smaller and less intimidating than Jericho had been. On paper, it looked like it would be a walk in the park. Israel's huge army against the little town of Ai would be like the Dallas Cowboys suiting up against a middle school B-team.

But Ai routed Israel's army, and thirty-six men of Israel lost their lives. Joshua was beside himself with shock, grief, and perplexity. The elders of Israel tore their clothes and heaped dust on their heads. Joshua fell down before the Lord and cried out, "Almighty LORD, why did you bring these people across the Jordan River? Was it to hand us over to the Amorites so that they could destroy us? I wish we had been content to live on the other side of the Jordan! Lord, what else can I say after Israel ran away from its enemy?" (Joshua 7:7-8, GW)

God replied, in effect, "Israel has sinned, and I'm not going to be with you or bless you or fight your battles for you until you deal with this sin."

At that point, Joshua and the elders didn't know who had sinned. But God knew and Achan knew. Achan thought he had gotten away with defying God, but as another scripture tells us, "The eyes of the LORD are in every place, keeping watch on the evil and the good" (Proverbs 15:3, ESV). God exposed Achan's sin, and the consequences were severe. Achan, his wife, and his children were stoned to death to purge the evil from Israel.

That reminds me of another lie of Satan. He will say, "This is only about you. This is your decision and yours alone. Nobody else has to be involved." But we have all seen how devastating this lie is in practice. If you are a man who commits adultery, will it affect your wife and your children? Yes, it will. Will it affect your children's children? It may very well touch their lives, too. Will it affect your coworkers, your neighbors, your church family, and people you may never meet? It will!

Sin is like a stone tossed into a still pond. The stone disappears, but ripple after ripple sweeps across the face of the water, touching even far shores.

The lie of the devil is that you can sin and get away with it. But you can't! I can't! No one can! Scripture tells us, "Whoever conceals their sins does not prosper, but the one who confesses and renounces them finds mercy." (Proverbs 28:13, NIV)

Third Discovery: The Devil Speaks *Twisted* Lies

In Genesis 3:4-5, the serpent tells Eve, "You will not surely die. For God knows that in the day you eat from it your eyes will be opened, and you will be like God, knowing good and evil."

Why is this a twisted lie? Because it's truth and falsehood mixed together. It's taking a bit of truth and intertwining it with a lie—like lacing a nice fruit punch with cyanide. It might look like fruit punch, smell like fruit punch, and even taste like fruit punch, but it is laced with death.

The devil loves to mix truth with error. He loves telling partial truths—a little bit of reliable information woven together with outright falsehood. But as the old saying goes, half-truth plus half-truth equals a whole lie! A half-truth, by definition, is a statement that mingles truth with falsehood, often with a deliberate intent to deceive. And that's what the devil does.

He says to Eve, "You're like a babe in the woods. You're like a little puppy, and your eyes haven't opened yet. If you eat this fruit, your eyes will really be opened." And what does it say in verses 6-7? "and she gave also to her husband with her, and he ate. Then the eyes of both of them were opened; and they knew that they were naked."

Yes, in that sense, Satan was right. Their eyes were opened—*but opened to what?*

Their eyes were opened because of sin, and sin will open your eyes to the three Ds—*darkness, degradation, and death.*

Suddenly, they knew they were naked. But what about that? They had always been naked. They were created naked, but they weren't aware of that fact at all. They hadn't even known it. Why hadn't they known it? *Because they didn't have self-consciousness, they had God-consciousness.* Since the very beginning, they had been looking to their Creator, not at themselves. They were looking at the animals, flowers, and vegetation in the garden, and all they had to do for the Lord. Everything was about the Lord; it wasn't about themselves.

But now, in a terrifying instant, all that changed. God-consciousness turned to self-consciousness. Their eyes were opened, "and they knew that they were naked."

Their eyes were open to darkness, degradation, humiliation, shame, and death. In the very next chapter of Genesis, they would experience the brutal death of their son, Abel, by the hand of their other son, Cain. Right away, they witnessed the bloody death of an innocent animal, killed so that God might clothe them with coats of animal skins. It became all too clear! *Sin brings death.* They died inside, and they unleashed death like a monstrous, never-ending plague in their once-perfect world. They began seeing things they wished they had never seen, hearing things they wished they had never heard, and learning things they wished they had never learned.

Now, here's the second twisted lie: Satan told Eve, "Your eyes will be opened, and you will be like God, knowing good and evil." He was saying, in effect, "Let's be honest, Eve. God's been holding out on you. If you eat that fruit, you will be like Him. And God doesn't want you to be like Him. God wants to hold all that for Himself. He wants to keep you on a short leash. But, man, if you eat of that tree, then you'll be like Him, knowing good and evil."

Satan was really speaking about the temptation that had snared *him*. It was he who had said, "I will make myself like the Most High" (Isaiah 14:14).

Now here's the truth: God *wants* you to be like Him! He doesn't want you to be *independent* of Him, but He wants you to be like Him. In 1 John 3:1-2 (NLT), we read these mind-blowing words: "See how very much our Father loves us, for he calls us his children, and that is what we are! But the people who belong to this world don't recognize that we are God's children because they don't know him. Dear friends, we are already God's children, but he has not yet shown us what we will be like when Christ appears. *But we do know that we will be like him,* for we will see him as he really is."

Your heavenly Father wants you to be like Him—just as a child is like his or her parent! Just as a little boy will copy the mannerisms of his daddy, or a little girl will imitate the way her mother does things. The Apostle Paul urges us to "be imitators of God, as beloved children. And walk in love, as Christ loved us" (Ephesians 5:1-2, ESV). The Lord wants you to be like Him in that you're holy, righteous, and walk in love.

But that's not what Satan was suggesting. He was suggesting that Eve could be her own god, knowing good and evil like God does. But we don't have the capacity to know good and evil like God does. He is the essence and very definition of holiness. The angels cry out in His presence, "Holy, Holy, Holy is the LORD of hosts, the whole earth is full of his glory!" (Isaiah 6:3). John tells us, "God is light, and in Him is no darkness at all" (1 John 1:5). God can discern even the slightest whiff of evil as He compares everything to His holiness.

You and I can't do that. And neither could Adam nor Eve. When their eyes were opened, they became self-conscious rather than God-conscious. They died in their spirit toward the LORD, just exactly like He warned it would happen. They couldn't evaluate good and evil through their own sinfulness, and neither can we—*apart from the Word of God and the indwelling Spirit of God.*

That's why it's so critical to be in God's Word every day. That's why it's so critical to walk under the guidance and in the fullness of God's Spirit. If we don't, we will surely fall under the deception of an enemy who is committed to harm us in every way he can.

But here's some fantastic news: "If we walk in the light, as He Himself is in the light, we have fellowship with one another, and the blood of Jesus His Son cleanses us from all sin." (1 John 1:7)

The World's Biggest Liar will keep spinning his subtle, blatant, and twisted deceptions and fake news until that day when the Lord silences him forever. But in the meantime, if we lean on the Lord through the days of our lives, we don't have to fall prey to his deceptions.

As believers in Jesus, we have the Holy Spirit living within us. He is the Spirit of truth, our Fake-News Detector, always alert and infinitely wise, at home in our very heart of hearts.

-3-

The World's Most Believed Lie

"There is a way which seems right to a person,
But its end is the way of death."

—PROVERBS 14:12

Does hell have a research and development department?

Probably not. But if it did, we might imagine a team of dark spirits working around the clock, devising new and ingenious lies to trip up, deceive, and confound each new generation of men and women on earth.

But I really don't think that's the case and here's why.

I think Satan has been recycling the same old, tired lies he used on our parents, grandparents, and great-grandparents, right back to the beginning of time. Why should he change what has been working so well when people keep right on believing the lies—the age-old, life-destroying falsehoods—of the devil?

Yes, he can dress up these deceptions in contemporary clothing, wrap them in today's jargon, and put them on Facebook, Snapchat, or in a Netflix movie, making them look new and edgy and cool. But they're basically the same time-worn, reconditioned lies he has used on us humans for years beyond counting.

In the last chapter, we talked about a gigantic one: *You can sin and get away with it.* That lie, when it was brand-new-out-of-the-box, worked with Eve in the Garden of Eden. And at this very moment, all over the world, millions of people are falling for it all over again.

Or how about this one: *If you want to be happy, you must put yourself first. You have to take care of Number One. Life is short, so go for the gusto.* The Son of God took on that lie Himself, telling His listeners in Matthew 10:39 (ESV): "Whoever finds his life will lose it, and whoever loses his life for my sake will find it." But right up to this instant in time, countless men and women are working very hard to please and promote themselves at the expense of others, elbowing their way to the front of the line to put themselves first. And it is making them utterly miserable, just as it has for untold multitudes down through the centuries. Instead of gaining life, they are losing it—and they're not even aware that it is draining away.

But there is one particular lie that the father of lies has used to great and devastating effect all over the world. Whole religions are based on it, and great temples have been built on its false foundation. It's as phony as a three-dollar-bill, but billions of people believe it anyway.

In fact, it's the most *believed* lie in the devil's huge arsenal of falsehoods. Even so, it remains dangerous, destructive, and damnable; a single lie that will send a soul to hell forever.

What is the world's most believed lie?

That an individual is saved, in part or in whole, by his or her good works. That good deeds and good works are essential to achieving eternal heaven.

A Great and Tragic Deception

This is the basis of every false religion and cult.

It is a religion of works, and in many ways it sounds good, plausible, and even commendable. But it's not true and never has been true. It is a flat-out lie.

There are huge and vastly wealthy cults in the United States of America that claim to believe in Jesus and trust Him for salvation. But underneath the nice-sounding spiritual glaze, they really teach a religion of works, and that good deeds, persistence, church membership, and hard work will somehow make you "worthy" or earn you a place in heaven.

Call me simple-minded, but I've always loved the little poem I heard from Adrian Rogers that says:

"I cannot work my soul to save;
That work my Lord has done;
But I will work like any slave
For the love of God's dear Son." [1]

You and I are not saved by works. No one is ever saved by works. The Bible makes this crystal clear in numerous passages (Ephesians 2:8-9; Titus 3:5; Galatians 2:16, 2:21; Romans 3:20, 3:28, and 11:6). Yet, people still believe that good works are the essential ingredient if you want to go to heaven. Deep down, they cling to the notion that somehow, somewhere, someday, God will weigh all their good works on a scale, and, with a little bit of good fortune, they will slip past Saint Peter at the pearly gates and squeak into heaven.

That's how so many people see salvation, but it's not that way at all. Not even close. In the book of Acts, one desperate man in the depths of a dungeon, on the razor-edge of suicide, fell trembling before Paul and Silas and asked the most important question in life: "Sirs, what must I do to be saved?" (Acts 16:30)

Consider that little word *do*.

"What must I DO to be saved?" People have been asking that question since Cain and Abel, and they are still asking it today. We think in terms of *do/doing*.

The Philippian jailer didn't even know where to start. He seemed to be saying, in effect, "I don't know a lot about you Jews. You have a lot

---

[1] Footnote: Adrian Rogers. "Totally Abandoned to the Gospel." Accessed online, 2024. https://www.lwf.org/pdfs/2041-Totally-Abandoned-to-the-Gospel-PTR.pdf.

Salvation by good works feels right. It adds up.

It sounds good. But it's a death trap!

of traditions and observances. What do I have to do? Do I have to get circumcised? Do I have to be baptized? Join a church? Tithe my income? Follow the law of Moses? Stop eating ham sandwiches? Tell me, what must I do to be saved?"

Most people in the world today think in those terms. They imagine salvation as some kind of cosmic merit system. They may not know much about God, but it seems logical to them that some way, somehow, you have to DO something. Because if you don't do it, you might not make it. And if God weighs your life on a scale and you come up short, you're done for.

I have a friend who was trying to share the gospel with his elderly grandfather. In response, the old man kept reciting the good deeds he had done in his life. One of his deeds was that back in the day, he had even put up a missionary family in his home for a week or two when they didn't have anywhere to stay. Surely God took notice of that, right!? That had to count!

Why do we, as human beings, naturally think that way—that our good deeds are powerful enough to "make us good"? Why do we imagine that salvation somehow rests on me, on my effort, and what I accomplish for God in the course of my life?

Let me suggest three reasons why we might think this way.

Reason 1: Salvation by Works Seems Right to the Human Heart

It just seems right. It makes sense to people. It sounds like a basic, logical conclusion: If you do more good than evil in your life, the heavenly scales will tip in your direction, and you will earn salvation and heaven. The Bible comments on this mindset in Proverbs 14:12 and again in Proverbs 16:25 (ERV):

> "There is a way that people think is right,
> but it leads only to death."

Salvation by good works feels right. It adds up. It sounds good. But it's a death trap!

Do you remember the shocking and devastating plane crash on Friday evening, July 16, 1999? John F. Kennedy Jr., his wife Carolyn, and her sister Lauren took off from Essex County Airport in New Jersey in his 1995 Piper Saratoga II to fly to Martha's Vineyard in Massachusetts. They were hurrying to get to his cousin's wedding scheduled for Saturday. The weather report was relatively decent—some haze in spots, but not insurmountable. Although Kennedy was not a greatly seasoned pilot, the short flight over the Atlantic Ocean seemed to him to be quite doable.

The plane took off a little after sunset. Visibility over the ocean proved to be more problematic than he anticipated. In such cases, spatial disorientation can easily occur. Investigators revealed that for some unknown reason, Kennedy had turned off the autopilot and began flying by sight and senses. Although the instrumentation on his state-of-the art aircraft was telling him he was descending, everything within him said the instruments were wrong. Approximately eight miles from his destination, he crashed into the ocean, killing all on board.[2]

The way that seemed so right to him was, in fact, so wrong. The way he chose ended in death. It was indeed tragic and heartbreaking.

As human beings created by God, we have been wired with an innate sense of justice. You can even hear a four-year-old protest with indignation, "It's not FAIR!" (And where did that sense of fairness come from?) Here is what our sense of justice tells us about life and the afterlife. *Bad people should be punished, and good people should be rewarded.* That's fair and just,

---

[2]Footnote: "Kennedy Plane Crash Investigation Report." *The New York Times*, July 7, 2000.

isn't it? Most of us don't like to watch movies and TV shows where the bad guy gets rewarded or gets away with greed and cruelty. We don't like it if the show ends and the bad dude walks off into the sunset, unharmed and unpunished. People can talk about 'anti-heroes' all they like, but deep down, we all want to see the villain get his comeuppance. We want to see the good guys and heroes come out on top.

When I was in high school and college, there was a popular movie character that I liked to watch. His name was Harry Callahan—Dirty Harry. It was one of Clint Eastwood's classic roles. This San Francisco homicide inspector wasn't going to put up with any shenanigans. Facing down the bad guys in a potential gun fight, he said things like, "You feeling lucky, punk?" Or maybe, "Go ahead, make my day!"

Why did we love him? Because he was on the side of law and order, standing against the city's sleazy underworld, the people who were willing to rob and rape and cheat and bully and kill. And in our hearts, we were cheering him on because the good guys need to win, and the bad guys need to lose. Evil needs to be punished, and noble deeds need to be rewarded. That's just how we think. That's our knee-jerk response.

Is that wrong? No, it's not wrong. But here's the problem. We tend to think of *ourselves* as the good people (who occasionally slip up and make 'mistakes'). But the Bible shows us a different reality. In the book of Romans, we read: "There is none righteous, not even one; there is none who understands, there is none who seeks for God; all have turned aside . . . There is none who does good, there is not even one." (Romans 3:10-12)

I vividly remember talking to my Catholic Aunt Regina about her husband, our beloved Uncle Harry. Uncle Harry was a Jewish man who didn't believe in Jesus. I spoke to Aunt Regina frankly about my concern for Uncle Harry's soul. He desperately needed Jesus Christ. But she just ended the uncomfortable conversation with these unforgettable words, "Well, Jeff, I just believe that heaven is a place for all good people."

So many people cling to this exact belief. It sounds right, doesn't it? But it is fatally flawed. You see, Jesus made it clear that "no one is good except God alone" (Mark 10:18). The very best of human beings is a no good, filthy sinner in desperate need of a Savior who can forgive and cleanse. Even though my Uncle Harry was a kind, generous, and respectable man, he was still a sinner. And like every other sinner, he was facing judgment and hell apart from Christ. Jesus said, "Therefore you are to be perfect, as your heavenly Father is perfect" (Matthew 5:48). Heaven is a perfect place intended for perfect people. Do you know any of those folks—perfect people? No! We are all imperfect sinners. The apostle Paul assures us that "**all** have sinned and fall short of the glory of God" (Romans 3:23). And do you know what "all" means in the Greek language? It means ALL.

So yes, good people should be rewarded—if only we could find any. And yes, again, bad people should be punished. But that means us, too—all of us. We have all fallen short and are under the righteous judgment of a Holy God.

In Isaiah chapter 6, Isaiah had a mind-blowing vision of the Lord:

"In the year of King Uzziah's death I saw the Lord sitting on a throne, lofty and exalted, with the train of his robe filling the temple. Seraphim stood above Him, each having six wings: with two he covered his face, and with two he covered his feet, and with two he flew. And one called out to another and said, "Holy, Holy, Holy, is the LORD of armies. The whole earth is full of His glory.'"

—Isaiah 6:1-3

Wow! What an experience! And how did the prophet respond to this awe-inspiring encounter with God? He cried out in fearful confession, "Woe is me, for I am ruined! Because I am a man of unclean lips, And I live among a people of unclean lips; For my eyes have seen the King, the LORD of hosts." (Isaiah 6:5)

> *Heaven is a perfect place intended for perfect people. Do you know any of those folks—perfect people? No! We are all imperfect sinners.*

Undone! Ruined! Doomed! Busted! I'm a sinner before a Holy God, and I wish I could somehow crawl under the floorboards to get away from His Holy gaze.

As you read further in his testimony, you discover that God Himself took care of Isaiah's sin and his dirty mouth. But that's the only way his sin could be removed. It required God's grace and provision in response to Isaiah's humble confession. The prophet could have never in a million years merited standing before a Holy God on his own. And neither can we.

Reason 2: Salvation by Works Appeals to Our Pride

Whatever it is, we like to think that we can do it.

In the interest of full disclosure, sometimes I don't like having my wife give me driving tips in the car. Even when I need them. Even when I might have wrecked the car without them. I just want to do it my way! When it comes to salvation, we do the same thing. We tell ourselves, "I've got this! Somehow, some way, I can grit my teeth, grind this out, and pull myself up by my bootstraps. I can earn this thing called salvation if I just try hard enough."

We have a tendency to think like that. But it doesn't matter what we think about the matter; the Bible presents crystal-clear truths. In Ephesians 2:8-9, we read: "For by grace you have been saved through faith; and that not of yourselves, it is the gift of God; not as a result of works, so that no one may boast."

Not by works. No one gets to boast.

If salvation really was by good works, if that could actually happen, heaven would be full of proud peacocks, strutting around and preening themselves. We'd say, "Well, it wasn't easy, but I applied myself, and now I've claimed the prize. I led a good life if I do say so myself, and that's why I'm in heaven."

But no one will ever say that in heaven. No one will utter words like that in front of God and His Holy Angels. All the praise for all eternity will be directed toward God, who saved us by His amazing, undeserved grace.

In Proverbs 6:16-17, Solomon gives us a list of seven things that God particularly hates. Number one on that list is a proud or haughty look. It's when someone looks down on someone else and feels superior to them in his or her heart. The New Testament says, "God is opposed to the proud, but gives grace to the humble." (James 4:6)

Salvation by works and achieving entry into heaven by a worthy life appeals to our sense of pride. We would like to think that God smiles on us because we're such nice people with good qualities and generous hearts. The sinful flesh loves to have its ego stroked. We love to have people "like" our pictures, posts, or thoughts on Instagram, Facebook, and X. It's an issue of human pride. The voice within us is constantly whispering, "Life is all about me, and I want what I want when I want it."

That sort of selfishness and self-centeredness *is* sin! It's interesting that the middle letter of the word S-I-N is "I." How appropriate since the heart of sin is truly the big "I." It's about what pleases me and what I get out of life along the way.

But here is the reverse of that. Here's the counterpoint.

It is salvation by grace through faith.

What does that realization do? It *humbles* the human soul, something that our sinful nature doesn't appreciate at all. The flesh doesn't want to be humbled. The flesh never orders a big slice of humble pie at a restaurant because we don't like to eat humble pie (or crow, for that matter). We don't like saying, "I couldn't do that," or "I'm unable," or "I was wrong."

In Luke 18, Jesus told a pointed story to a group of religious leaders who were particularly full of themselves. One translation described them as men who were "complacently pleased with themselves over their moral performance and looked down their noses at the common people." (MSG)

The story went like this:

"Two men went up into the temple to pray, one a Pharisee and the other a tax collector. The Pharisee stood and was praying this to himself: 'God, I thank You that I am not like other people: swindlers, unjust, adulterers, or even like this tax collector. I fast twice a week; I pay tithes of all that I get.' But the tax collector, standing some distance away, was even unwilling to lift up his eyes to heaven, but was beating his breast, saying, 'God, be merciful to me, the sinner!' I tell you, this man went to his house justified rather than the other; for everyone who exalts himself will be humbled, but he who humbles himself will be exalted."

—Luke 18:10-14

The King James translation of this passage says that the Pharisee "prayed thus with himself." He might as well have been praying to himself because his prayers never rose higher than the ceiling. He was saying in effect, "Lord, You ought to be so glad that You have me as a follower. Look at all my good works! *Oh, what a good boy am I!*"

But in contrast, the tax collector wouldn't even lift his eyes toward the Lord. He was so filled with anguish and grief over his sin that he was pounding his own chest with his fist. And if you had a microphone and put it very near his downcast head, you would have heard, through his tears, this prayer of heartfelt contrition: "God have mercy on me. I'm such a terrible sinner!"

Jesus wrapped up His story by saying that the tax collector went home justified—cleansed of heart and right with God—while the Pharisee just went home. Why? Because the tax collector understood there was none righteous, not even one. He understood that he didn't deserve anything, and he was casting himself on the mercy of God.

Did the Lord's story make any impact on those proud religious leaders? The Bible doesn't say. But it isn't easy to see your desperate need for God when you are totally full of yourself. *Salvation by good works appeals to the pride and sinful nature in all of us.*

Reason 3: Salvation by Works Seems to Have a Biblical Basis

People who believe in salvation by works turn quickly to the New Testament book of James for support. People have been doing this very thing for centuries, which seemed to get under the skin of Martin Luther.

Luther, you may remember, was a monk in the fifteenth and sixteenth centuries who started the Protestant Reformation. He was the one who tried so hard by his good works to please God. He would deliberately sleep in freezing cold conditions without a blanket. He would take a whip and beat himself on his back, desperately trying to earn God's favor. He was the one who said that if heaven could be earned by being a good monk, then he would have surely earned heaven.

That's what made it so jaw-dropping when the actual truth dawned on him: You can't earn your way to heaven. No one can, and no one ever has. No monk, no priest, no pastor, and no pope. It all began when Luther was reading Romans chapter 1. (By the way, if you don't like life change, then the Bible could be a dangerous book for you.) Luther's eyes rested for a moment on Romans 1:17:

"But the righteous man shall live by faith."

Yes, it is faith alone that saves, but faith alone is never faith alone. It is always accompanied with action. True saving faith is never without authenticating works.

Boom! From that time forward, Martin Luther could never unread that verse or unthink the thoughts that suddenly exploded in his soul. As God's Spirit enlightened his heart and mind, Luther realized that salvation is not about good works. It's not about trying harder and harder. It's not about working your fingers to the bone or putting yourself through intense suffering to somehow please God and merit His acceptance. Salvation is about trusting in the Lord and His provision for our sin.

Did that divine revelation change his life? Yes, it did. In fact, it changed the whole world.

Even so, brilliant man that he was, Martin Luther had problems with the Book of James. In his mind, some of the things James wrote seemed to contradict the words of the Apostle Paul. In James 2:17, we read: "Even so faith, if it has no works, is dead, being by itself."

Luther understood those words of James as an attack on salvation by grace through faith. But here is where he missed the point: Yes, it is faith alone that saves, but faith alone is never faith alone. It is always accompanied with action. True saving faith *is never without authenticating works.* James 2:18 goes on to tell us, "But someone may *well* say, "You have faith and I have works; show me your faith without the works, and I will show you my faith by my works."

Here is a helpful way to understand this: Faith is the **ROOT** of salvation, and works are the **FRUIT** of salvation. Works don't produce salvation, salvation produces works! Good works grow organically out of your salvation like sweet apples on a healthy apple tree.

In Ephesians 2:8-10 we read: "For by grace you have been saved through faith; and that not of yourselves, it is the gift of God; not as a result of works, so that no one may boast. For we are His workmanship, created in Christ Jesus for good works, which God prepared beforehand so that we would walk in them."

Let's focus on three simple words in this passage that will help us all keep our theology straight with regard to salvation.

First: We are saved **BY** grace.

Second: We are saved **THROUGH** faith.

Third: We are saved **FOR** good works.

By grace, *through* faith, *for* good works.

Grace is God's love in action. It is the undeserved, unmerited, unearned favor of God. Grace is like electricity that comes to your house. Obviously, if you don't have electricity, you can't run an appliance. You can't make toast or dry your hair or turn on the TV. If you do have electricity in your home, however, all those electrical devices will work just fine—*as long as you plug them in.* If grace is electricity, then faith is plugging into that electricity.

You won't get toast without electricity, and you still won't get toast unless you plug in the toaster. But if you plug in the toaster at that live electrical outlet, you get beautiful, golden-brown toast. In the same way, we are saved BY grace THROUGH faith. When we plug our humble faith into God's amazing grace, salvation comes to our heart!

The next verse, Ephesians 2:10, then speaks of good works. You see, we are not saved *by* good works, we are saved *for* good works. God has good works that He wants each of us to accomplish with all the talents, skills, and opportunities He provides for us. Are we allowing Him to work through us? Is His grace flowing through our faith accomplishing anything good in the world?

Here is the acid test to see if you have truly been saved: Have you been changed from the inside out? If you're still the same old, mean, bitter, lustful, greedy, nasty person that you've always been, then the truth is you have not been saved. True salvation changes everything in your life moving forward. You become a new creature, a new creation (2 Corinthians 5:17). It is impossible to stay the same once you truly come to Christ by grace through faith. And your friends and family will begin to notice the difference. They will begin to recognize that your countenance, your attitude, your words, your outlook—everything is different now.

As the Apostle James put it, "But someone may *well* say, 'You have faith and I have works; show me your faith without the works, and I will show you my faith by my works'" (James 2:18). True faith always produces good works.

Salvation is by Christ's Work—through
the Cross and the Empty Tomb

Let's go back for a minute to that Philippian jailer in Acts chapter 16. He's just experienced an earthquake so violent that all the iron doors in his prison have been shaken loose and swung open. Knowing that he will be executed in shame if his prisoners escape, he's almost to the point of taking his own life with a sword.

That's where we pick up the story in Acts 16:28-34:

"But Paul cried out with a loud voice, saying, "Do not harm yourself, for we are all here!" And he called for lights and rushed in, and trembling with fear he fell down before Paul and Silas, and after he brought them out, he said, "Sirs, what must I do to be saved?"

They said, "Believe in the Lord Jesus, and you will be saved, you and your household." And they spoke the word of the Lord to him together with all who were in his house. And he took them that very hour of the night and washed their wounds, and immediately he was baptized, he and all his household. And he brought them into his house and set food before them, and rejoiced greatly, having believed in God with his whole household."

Salvation is Christ's work that He accomplished on the cross and through the empty tomb. So, what do you need to do to receive salvation? You don't need to *do* anything. You simply need to believe and receive.

In Islam, you must follow the Five Pillars of Islam. In Buddhism, you have to follow the Eightfold Path. And so it is in every other religion or cult. They give you a list of things you have to *do*. Christianity is different from all other religions because Christianity is not spelled D-O; it's spelled D-O-N-E. It is finished! Jesus has paid the full price for our salvation through His death and resurrection.

So, what must I do to be saved?

Paul told the Philippian jailer, "Believe on the Lord Jesus, and you will be saved, you and your household" (Acts 16:31 NKJV). That's a good statement. But what specifically are we to believe about Him?

First of all, *believe who He is*. As Peter declared, "You are the Christ, the Son of the living God!" (Matthew 16:16)

In John chapter 9, Jesus healed a man who had been born blind—which made the religious leaders upset and angry. (They didn't approve of anything they couldn't control.) After they hauled the man in for questioning and then angrily threw him out of the synagogue, he had another encounter with the Lord.

Christianity is different from all other religions because Christianity is not spelled D-O; it's spelled D-O-N-E. It is finished! Jesus has paid the full price for our salvation through His death and resurrection.

Pastor Jeff

"Jesus heard that they had put him out, and finding him, He said, "Do you believe in the Son of Man?" He answered, "Who is He, Lord, that I may believe in Him?" Jesus said to him, "You have both seen Him, and He is the one who is talking with you." And he said, "Lord, I believe." And he worshiped Him."

—John 9:35-38

The Jews of that day knew very well that you don't worship a man. You worship God and God only. But this man worshiped Jesus. Why? *Because Jesus Christ is God, that's why!* That truth alone knocks the foundation out from under every cult or false religion under the sun. You see, every cult and every false religion has the same DNA; they all reject the full deity of Jesus Christ.

Jesus Christ is fully God and fully man, co-equal with God the Father. So that's the first thing you believe about Him. You believe who He is for Jesus said, "And you will die in your sins if you do not believe that I AM WHO I AM." (John 8:34 GNB)

Secondly, *you believe what He has done.* Paul told the Corinthians: "For I delivered to you as of first importance what I also received, that Christ died for our sins according to the Scriptures, and that He was buried, and that He was raised on the third day according to the Scriptures." (1 Corinthians 15:3-4)

That is the gospel. It's His death, it's His burial, it's His resurrection. Christianity says that Jesus is God, that He died on the cross for our sins, and that He rose again from the dead. Jesus Christ is the only founder of faith who died and came back to life. The founder of Islam is Mohammad. He's dead! The founder of Buddhism is Gautama Buddha. He's dead! But Jesus is alive forevermore. And He says, "Follow Me!" You can follow Him—the Son of God and God the Son—who is alive at this very moment and holds the keys of death and hell. (Revelation 1:18)

Here's the truth: If you are in Christ today, you can know that you are forgiven, and that your name is written in the Lamb's Book of Life.

The great trouble with Satan's most believed lie that salvation is a result of good works is simply this: How much is enough? How many good deeds, good thoughts, good actions, and good prayers does it take? And what if you fall one good deed short of the requirement? How terrible that would be!

But it's all a lie of the devil.

Here's the truth: If you are in Christ today, you can know that you are forgiven, and that your name is written in the Lamb's Book of Life. You can know beyond all doubt that if you died today, you would be in heaven with Jesus.

Years ago, when I was a freshman at the University of Texas in Austin, I went to the laundromat with a friend of mine. He was Catholic. As we were waiting on our clothes to dry, I asked him the diagnostic Evangelism Explosion question, "Do you know for sure that if you died today, you'd go to heaven?"

"No, I don't," he said. "And furthermore, *you* don't know either!"

"Oh?" I replied. "I don't?"

"No! Nobody can know that. You only find out the answer to that question when you die. And after you're dead, then you will know if you made it or you didn't." My friend believed the devil's most pernicious lie that salvation is a result of works. He had no assurance of his eternal destiny because he didn't know how many good works it would actually take for him to merit heaven.

I can't remember how the conversation concluded. But I do remember that the Lord gave me the right Scripture to quote at that very moment. It was 1 John 5:11-13:

> "And the testimony is this, that God has given us eternal life, and this life is in His Son. He who has the Son has the life; he who does not have the Son of God does not have the life. These things I have written to you who believe in the name of the Son of God, so that you may **know** that you have eternal life."

God does not promise us a *hope so, guess so, maybe so* salvation. He gives to us a *know so* salvation! And you can *know so* today, if you will believe on the Lord Jesus Christ.

We've all heard about the sinking of the Titanic back in 1912 and some of the stories that came out of that great tragedy. One of the most striking stories to me was the account a young Scotsman named Aquila Webb gave in a church service in Hamilton, Ontario, four years after that disaster.

The young man had been pulled from the sea and was giving his testimony in front of the church. One of the young man's fellow passengers on the ship was a godly pastor named John Harper, who was traveling to Chicago to minister at Moody Church. He was also from Scotland and was traveling with his daughter and sister.

After the Titanic hit the iceberg and began to sink in the frigid waters of the North Atlantic, Harper began to witness to everybody he could—even as he made sure that the women and children got on the boats.

When the ship finally sank, Harper had only a piece of wreckage to keep him afloat in the icy sea.

At the church in Hamilton, the young Scotsman told the congregation: "I was John Harper's last convert!" Drifting on another piece of wreckage, the sea brought Pastor John Harper close to Aquila Webb. The pastor called out, "Man, are you saved?"

God does not promise us a hope so, guess so, maybe so salvation. He gives to us a know so salvation! And you can know so today, if you will believe on the Lord Jesus Christ.

"No, no, I'm not," the younger man replied. The pastor answered, "Believe on the Lord Jesus Christ, and you shall be saved."

The waves separated them, but a short time later, they drifted together again. Again, John Harper called out, "Are you saved now?"

"No," Webb answered, "I can't honestly say that I am.'" And Harper said to him, again, "Believe on the Lord Jesus Christ, and you shall be saved." Shortly after that, Harper disappeared into the dark sea. And Webb told the congregation in Canada, "There, alone in the night, and with two miles of ocean underneath me, I believed, and I was saved."[3]

Satan's big lie is that good works will save you.

That young Scotsman didn't have any time to pile up good works. All he could do was call on the name of Jesus for salvation.

It was enough.

And it still is.

---

[3]Footnote: William R. Moody. *The Titanic's Last Hero: A Story of John Harper.* (Wolgemuth & Hyatt Publishers, 1997.)

-4-

Spinning Your Circumstances

*"I am convinced that life is 10% what happens
to me and 90% how I react to it."*
—CHUCK SWINDOLL

Forrest Gump was a colossal hit for Paramount Studios in 1994, raking in over 680 million dollars worldwide.

That iconic movie, you may remember, chronicled the life of one slow-witted, kind-hearted, athletically-gifted man, portrayed by Tom Hanks. He was a stud on the Alabama Crimson Tide football team, playing for Bear Bryant as a running back. He was a ping-pong champion, amazing audiences worldwide with his abilities. And when he served in Vietnam, he won the Congressional Medal of Honor for saving almost his entire platoon when they were attacked.

He also saved the life of Lieutenant Dan Taylor. But as it turned out, Lt. Dan wasn't so glad about being saved.

One key scene in the movie depicts a powerful interaction between Forrest Gump and Lt. Dan Taylor as they were convalescing in the hospital. Lt. Dan, who was severely injured and lost both his legs in combat, confronts Forrest about saving his life during battle.

The conversation reveals Lt. Dan's deep emotional turmoil, his feelings that God had cheated him, and his loss of hope for a promising future. Lt. Dan saw himself as a legless freak with no honor and no purpose. He expresses anger and frustration towards Forrest for saving him and robbing him of the glory of having died in combat, faithfully serving his country. In his mind, his identity and future have been irreparably altered.

Forrest, true to his character, responds with simple honesty. He tells Lt. Dan that the fact that he's in a wheelchair doesn't change who he was made to be. Forrest's straightforward reply highlights the contrast between Lt. Dan's complex emotional state and Forest's more uncomplicated view of life.

To be sure, Lt. Dan had experienced some very traumatic and difficult circumstances. But even after the horrific events of Vietnam faded into the rearview mirror, he was still filled with anger, bitterness, frustration, and grief. It wasn't getting better for him; it was getting worse.

What about you? How do you respond to the difficulties that come into your life? Do you respond like Lt. Dan, lashing out in anger? Do you become jaded, bitter, and cynical because of the hurts and devastations that you have endured? Do you find yourself blaming others for your difficulties? Or maybe blaming God?

None of us makes it through this life unscarred. Circumstances are what they are, and none of us can dodge them. When Jesus said, "In the world, you *will* have tribulation," He meant what He said. The bad things that happen to us in life are real and not part of Satan's fake news. In *Forrest Gump,* Lt. Dan really did lose his legs in battle. That became his reality for the rest of his life.[1]

So, where does the devil come into this?

He comes alongside us at the worst, most vulnerable season in our lives and puts his own spin on our circumstances. He tells us what to think about them and how to feel about them.

But here's the thing: He is lying.

---

[1] Footnote: *Forrest Gump*. Directed by Robert Zemeckis. Paramount Pictures, 1994.

He will say things like this: "See, this proves that God doesn't love you or even care about you. He's lost your file, man! If He's so 'good' why did He allow this to happen to you? Your situation is proof positive that it's foolish, futile, and stupid to praise, trust, and worship God."

Sometimes, when our highways are being repaired, the road crew likes to work at night under lights to avoid the heavy traffic. And that's when Satan and his demons like to work as well. They like shadowed days, black nights, and dark, even tragic, circumstances. These evil ones are attracted to your grief, disappointment, and despair like moths drawn to a streetlight at dusk. Why? Because they see a real opportunity to pry you away from your relationship with the living God who loves you.

In this chapter, we're going to zero in on a powerful, often neglected portion of Scripture that was written mostly in the dark—until it was bathed in a sudden, unexpected river of light. It's in the third chapter of the Book of Lamentations.

The Book No One Wants to Read

Lamentations was written by the prophet Jeremiah. It's just five chapters long, but when most people run across it in their Bible reading, they often want to skip past it. They will say, "I'm not sure I want to read that book. It sounds kind of depressing. I think I will get into the Psalms—or maybe the gospel of John."

And yet (as we will see), there is a very strong dose of divine encouragement in this book that makes wading through the sadness more than worthwhile. The word *lamentations* comes from a Latin word that speaks of "funeral dirges." The dictionary defines it as: "The passionate expression of grief or sorrow." That's what it means to lament. And that's certainly what Jeremiah is all about in the Book of Lamentations.

If you think you have a tough job, consider Jeremiah's career. Clearly called by God in his youth to be a prophet to God's people, he doggedly

Do you view God through the lens of your bad circumstances, or do you view your bad circumstances through the lens of God?

kept at it for forty years—with virtually no response and no change of heart among the people. But he got up every morning, carried his lunch box to work, and told that cynical crowd, "You guys need to turn around. You need to respond to the Lord. You need to repent and get things right with God. And if you don't, judgment is coming."

But they didn't listen. They wanted no part of this man's message. In fact, they wanted to kill him. Even so, whether they liked it or not, Jeremiah was truly God's spokesman, and all the shocking disasters he predicted in the name of the Lord truly came to pass.

This is how the events unfolded for Judah.

Nebuchadnezzar was king of Babylon, the superpower of that day. With their fast and powerful army, the Babylonians had already humiliated and dominated the nation of Judah. So, when the foolish king of Judah decided to rebel against this world colossus (ignoring Jeremiah's strong warnings against doing so), it was only a matter of time until Nebuchadnezzar sent his troops to annihilate them in response.

The Babylonian army besieged Jerusalem for over a year, not allowing anyone in or out. Then, when the Jewish people were starving, the invaders finished their siege ramps, broke down the wall of the city, and came pouring in like a torrent of angry wasps. They pushed down all the walls around the city and completely destroyed the beautiful temple Solomon had built to house and honor the Lord. Without mercy, Nebuchadnezzar's soldiers slaughtered multitudes of men, women, and children and took thousands as captives. Anything and everything of value, they carted away to Babylon.

Jeremiah was left alone among the ruins and the ashes.

He was lonely, heartsick, and filled with grief as he surveyed what was left of Jerusalem, the holy city. No wonder he wrote a book called "Lamentations." All he could do was weep because the devastation was so great.

So where does that encouragement I spoke of make its appearance?

In fact, it pops up unexpectedly right in the middle of the disaster. It's like a beautiful, fragile flower that grows up through a crack in the asphalt.

The prophet Jeremiah is a true man of God with a strong faith and a good heart. But he's still suffering. He's still agonizing over what happened to his country and people. He is mourning, and that mourning is neither inappropriate nor out of place.

But that mourning needs to be under the protection of God's Holy Spirit because this is also a time of spiritual danger. We will see the devil move in on Jeremiah in his pain, just as he moves in on you and me in our times of disappointment and suffering. We are going to see what goes on in Jeremiah's heart and how he turns the tables on the devil in a surprising and unexpected reversal.

Here is the big question for us in this chapter: *Do you view God through the lens of your bad circumstances, or do you view your bad circumstances through the lens of God?*

What follows is a taste of what this godly man felt in this darkest moment of his life. It's not fun reading, but it sets the context for what is to come.

"I am the man who has seen affliction
Because of the rod of His wrath.
He has driven me and made me walk
In darkness and not in light.

Surely against me He has turned His hand
Repeatedly all the day.
He has caused my flesh and my skin to waste away,
He has broken my bones.
He has besieged and encompassed me with bitterness and hardship.
In dark places He has made me dwell,
Like those who have long been dead.
He has walled me in so that I cannot go out;
He has made my chain heavy.
Even when I cry out and call for help,
He shuts out my prayer.
He has blocked my ways with hewn stone;
He has made my paths crooked.
He is to me like a bear lying in wait,
Like a lion in secret places.
He has turned aside my ways and torn me to pieces;
He has made me desolate.
He bent His bow
And set me as a target for the arrow.
He made the arrows of His quiver
To enter into my inward parts.
I have become a laughingstock to all my people,
Their mocking song all the day.
He has filled me with bitterness,
He has made me drunk with wormwood.
He has broken my teeth with gravel;
He has made me cower in the dust.
My soul has been rejected from peace;
I have forgotten happiness."

—Lamentations 3:1-17

In the following pages, I want you to notice three crucial insights concerning this portion of God's Word.

First: Satan Wants Us to See God as Mean, Cruel, and Sadistic

When you find yourself in a dark time, a lonely time, or a season of hurt, pain, or fear, the father of lies wants you to take out your pencil and do a dot-to-dot. He wants you to draw lines between your unhappy circumstances and the God who *allows* those hurtful times to enter your life.

He wants you to conclude that God has a mean streak—that He actually enjoys watching you struggle and thrash about in that dark and narrow place. He wants you to conclude that God isn't as good and kind and loving as you thought He was—in fact, He might even be a little bit sadistic.

Jeremiah really shares from the heart in this passage. In some ways, it reminds me of the Book of Psalms. One of the reasons I love the Psalms is because these ancient Hebrew poems are so transparent, honest, and true to life. King David and the other writers will tell you just what they are feeling and what's going on inside their souls. Jeremiah does the same thing in this chapter.

Circumstances and feelings always fit together. Have you noticed that?

We all like the word "happy," and we've probably sung or heard "Happy Birthday" ten thousand times in our lives. But what does the word really mean? Happy comes from a shorter word, H-A-P, *hap,* which means "an occurrence, a happening." We get the word *happenstance* from the root word *hap.* So, in the course of our lives, we're pleased when we have good happenings, good occurrences. In such times, we describe ourselves as 'happy.' Why are we happy? Because we've got good *hap.* Things are rolling along well for us. The weather's great, we've had plenty to eat, and as the old song goes, everything's coming up roses.

You win the lottery—and I'm not endorsing this—but you're happy, right? You get a promotion at work, you're happy. Somebody comes to

We are never more vulnerable to Satan's

fake news than when we are in pain, grief,

or deeply trying circumstances.

your house and says, "I just felt led to give you 100,000 dollars." Wow! That's a very good hap. And if your hap is good, you're happy.

But what takes place when your hap is bad—when things go sideways in your life and you lose your job or your health or your marriage or a loved one? You are unhappy, because your hap is bad.

Reading in the Contemporary English Version, Jeremiah says:

"I cannot find peace or remember happiness.
I tell myself, "I am finished! I can't count on the LORD to do anything for me."
Just thinking of my troubles and my lonely wandering makes me miserable.
That's all I ever think about, and I am depressed."

—Lamentations 3:17-20

Jeremiah is saying, "All I see is devastation 24/7. My circumstances are awful—and so are my feelings!" And then . . . watch out! At our weakest moments, the devil moves in to take advantage of the situation.

We are never more vulnerable to Satan's fake news than when we are in pain, grief, or deeply trying circumstances. This is when the devil likes to move in and say, "You see that? You can't trust God. He's not good. He doesn't love you. Look around you. Just check out what's going on in your life."

Our circumstances and feelings become the devil's workshop. The "spin doctor" goes to work with your troubles and heartaches, spinning them so that you will think negatively about God and develop a warped view of Him. And that's what happens to Jeremiah.

There's no doubt about it: The prophet is having a terrible time with the Lord in these first twenty verses.

In Lamentations 3:7-8, we read: "He has walled me in so that I cannot go out; He has made my chain heavy. Even when I cry out and call for help, He shuts out my prayer."

Another translation says, "Even when I cry out and plead for help, he locks up my prayers and throws away the key" (Lamentations 3:8, MSG). In other words, "Lord, I'm in big time trouble here, but You don't seem to be hearing me at all. I think my prayers are just bouncing off the ceiling."

In verses 10-11 of that same chapter, Jeremiah writes: "He is to me like a bear lying in wait, like a lion in secret places. He has turned aside my ways and torn me to pieces; He has made me desolate."

We like to think of God walking with us and giving us comfort, but to this grieving prophet, God's presence had become terrifying. Why does he say such harsh things about the Lord? Because that's how he *feels*. His circumstances are bad, and his feelings match right up with them. What an opportune time for the devil to come in with his fake news.

The devil was saying to him, "Yeah, that's right, Jeremiah. You've had a great life ever since God called you, right? What a joke! Now, just look around you. Look at those smoking ruins. Look at the devastation and the dead bodies. Your life couldn't get any worse. This is proof positive that trusting God and being His spokesman gets you nowhere!"

Mark it down: the devil wants us to see God as mean and cruel and sadistic.

But that's only the beginning of what he wants.

Second: The Devil Wants Us to Lose Hope

Once you believe the lie that God is cruel and sadistic—once you conclude that the only one with the power to save you doesn't really care—well, then, you just throw in the towel. You give up on life.

Jeremiah had started down that road. At that moment, God seemed to him as random and cruel as a marauding wild bear waiting to tear him apart. Where was the God who had known him before he was born and had chosen him in the womb to be His servant? Where was the companion who had walked with him through his youth? This is the God who seemingly filled him with bitterness and gave him gravel sandwiches for lunch. (Lamentations 3:15-16)

In verse 18, he sums it up with these dark words: "My strength has perished, and so has my hope from the LORD." Another translation puts it in these stark words: "I no longer have any hope that the LORD will help me." (ERV)

Jeremiah's circumstances and feelings had merged together like two dark rivers, and that was the moment Satan chose to strike with his fake news broadcast. "That's right, Jeremiah! There's no hope. All the avenues are closed. It's hopeless. You might as well curl up in a fetal position and die like everyone else."

It reminds me of the moment when terrible circumstances and broken emotions overwhelmed the wife of Job, and she blurted out, "Do you still hold fast your integrity? Curse God and die!" (Job 2:9). Did she really mean that? Probably not. She and Job had been together through thick and thin. But in her most vulnerable moment, the adversary had whispered dark and despairing words into her soul.

I'm reminded of a man who used to be in the news quite frequently. His nickname was 'Dr. Death.' Before his passing in 2011, Jack Kevorkian was a public champion and spokesman for a terminal patient's 'right to die' by physician-assisted suicide. During his career, he claimed to have helped 130 people end their lives.

When someone in a terminal situation, possibly dealing with pain, would call him, Dr. Death would hurry right over with his IVs full of poison and kill them. Conservative radio host Rush Limbaugh sarcastically called him 'Jack the Dripper.'[2]

Why would anyone call on a 'doctor' like Jack Kevorkian, the doctor of death?

Because when you lose hope, you lose your desire to go on. You tell yourself, "It's never going to get any better. There's no way out of this." In fact, that's the reason so many people, even healthy people, with all kinds of potential, take their own lives. They simply lose hope.

In 1972, an Irish singer named Gilbert O'Sullivan had a mega-hit song called "Alone Again, Naturally." It was the number one tune on America's pop charts for six weeks.[3]

And the song was about as dark as they come.

It begins with O'Sullivan's determination to throw himself off a tower and then goes into all the reasons why he is so depressed and hopeless. He was jilted at the altar, his dad died, his mom was shattered and lonely, and in the process, O'Sullivan lost his faith. The reality of life had cut him to pieces, *"Leaving me to doubt all about God and His mercy . . . For if He really does exist, why did He desert me in my hour of need . . . ?"*

When it first came out, that song became embedded in my brain and heart. I was eleven years old, and my mom and dad were having marital problems. Then, my dad packed up and left. I can still remember riding with my mom in the car, tears streaming down her cheeks, and hearing that depressing song on the radio.

"In my hour of need, I truly am, indeed, alone again, naturally."

Gilbert O'Sullivan no doubt went on to a fine career as a singer and entertainer. But those song lyrics came right out of hell. They were nothing

---

[2]Footnote: Neal Nicol and Harry Wylie. *Between the Dying and the Dead: Dr. Jack Kevorkian's Life and the Battle to Legalize Euthanasia.* (Madison: University of Wisconsin Press, 2006.)
[3]Footnote: Gilbert O'Sullivan, "Alone Again (Naturally)," recorded 1972, [track number] on [album title], MAM, [access type].

> *God is a God of hope! He overflows with it!*
>
> *And He loves to give you hope.*

but devastating fake news. And that's what the devil specializes in doing. He slips in the back door of your mind in your hour of greatest need and says, " Where is God in all this? And you say He's a God of mercy? Seriously? He's left you! He's not here for you. You're all alone. Why don't you just admit it? Why don't you just curse God and die!?"

And in those terrible moments when your heart feels like it will break apart in your chest, the devil will take the light that you have for the Lord, the candle that you have burning for Jesus, and try to blow it out. He will work diligently to try to extinguish your hope and vaporize your faith. He wants to hear you say, as Jeremiah said in Lamentations 3:18, "My strength is perished and so has my hope from the LORD."

Listen! When you lose hope, you lose everything. You lose your desire to go on. But why do you lose hope? The answer is simple. You lose hope *because you lose sight of God.*

One of my favorite verses in all of the New Testament comes near the end of the book of Romans. In chapter 15, verse 13, Paul writes, "Now may the God of hope fill you with all joy and peace in believing, so that you will abound in hope by the power of the Holy Spirit." (Romans 15:13)

Another translation renders it like this:

> "Now may God, the fountain of hope, fill you to overflowing with uncontainable joy and perfect peace as you trust in him. And may the power of the Holy Spirit continually surround your life with his super-abundance until you radiate with hope!" (TPT)

God is a God of hope! He overflows with it! And He loves to give you hope. The Holy Spirit loves to fill up your hope tank until it overflows and splashes on those around you. But Satan and his demonic cohorts seek to stick a hose into that tank and siphon it away. And they were doing a pretty good job of it with Jeremiah, God's chief spokesman.

That sad Irish singer, Gilbert O'Sullivan, had only one real note in his dark ballad: despair. From the first words of those lyrics to the last, it was depressing doom and gloom.

But not so with Jeremiah.

In the book of Lamentations, there is a turning point—one of the greatest turning points in all of Scripture. Listen to this, and be amazed:

"Surely my soul remembers
This I recall to my mind,
Therefore I have hope.
The LORD's lovingkindnesses indeed never cease,
For His compassions never fail.
They are new every morning;
Great is Your faithfulness.
"The LORD is my portion," says my soul,
"Therefore I have hope in Him."
The LORD is good to those who wait for Him,
To the person who seeks Him.
It is good that he waits silently
For the salvation of the LORD.

—Lamentations 3:20-26

Wow! *Did you hear that?* What a comeback! Jeremiah had been looking around at all the rubble, devastation, and dead bodies—all the awful, horrific things that came with the destruction of Jerusalem. And that's all that he could see. In those sickening moments, his emotions trailed right along with his awful circumstances. But then he suddenly remembered: "Hey, I've been looking down all this time. I need to quit looking down and start looking up!"

And when he did, he saw the Lord—His friend, companion, savior, and deliverer. This same dynamic is true to this very day. Satan wants you to think that God is mean and sadistic—or at least distant and uncaring. He wants you to dwell on those thoughts until your faith and hope begin to drain away.

But God wants something else.

Third: God Wants You to Fix Your Eyes on Him and See the Truth

If we're being honest, it's way too easy to fix our eyes on our circumstances. I can still vividly remember a time in my life when I took my eyes off the Lord and focused on my seemingly impossible circumstances. Early in 2003, God laid the idea of starting From His Heart Ministries on my heart. The church I pastored, First Baptist Church Texarkana, already had a TV ministry, but it was only broadcast locally on the NBC affiliate in Shreveport, LA. I felt God's leading to expand the television outreach of my preaching from local to national. I talked with several close friends, and they sensed that God was in this. So, in November of 2004, I founded From His Heart Ministries, a stand-alone 501(c)(3) non-profit corporation. Two friends provided the seed money of $35,000 to get the ministry off the ground. I naively thought I was adequately financed for the path ahead. When I attended my first National Religious Broadcasters Convention in Los Angeles, CA, in February of 2005, I learned very quickly that starting a national media ministry would require a lot more than $35,000. I was told by a trusted friend in the business that the cost to successfully get From His Heart Ministries up and running would be around $500,000—a half million! When I heard that staggering number, I was instantly deflated and ready to throw in the towel and walk away. How on earth was I going to raise that much money? It seemed impossible. Then I started to really question if I had even heard God correctly.

I left that convention thinking the dream was dead. From His Heart Ministries would never succeed. The financial obstacles were too insurmountable. I was in despair and defeat because my eyes were focused on the problem and not the problem-solver, whose name is Jesus.

Over the next few weeks, God continued to speak His truth to my heart in my quiet time with Him. He reminded me that He is the God of might and miracles. Where He guides, He also provides. What was impossible for me to do was not impossible for Him to do. He is the God "who is able to do exceeding abundantly beyond all that we ask or think" (Ephesians 3:19). He is the God of the impossible! Truly, the word *impossible* should be viewed as *I'm possible* with God.

The Lord convicted me of having such little faith. As I repented and sought His forgiveness, I prayed these words: "God, I don't know how the money will come for this ministry, but I know you are able, and I trust You to bring it to pass. From His Heart Ministries is not about me; it is all about you!"

And guess what happened? Within two weeks of trusting God for provision, I received an unsolicited check in the mail for $100,000. A few weeks after that, I received another check for $100,000. Then the Missions Committee at First Baptist Texarkana voted to provide another $100,000 in support. By God's grace and provision, the $35,000 startup money grew by $300,000, and From His Heart Ministries was cleared for takeoff. How quickly the situation changed when I took my eyes off my circumstances and trusted my King.

And that's what Jeremiah does. In words that have been immortalized in song after song, hymn after hymn, the prophet declared: "The LORD's lovingkindnesses indeed never cease, for His compassions never fail. They are new every morning; great is Your faithfulness. 'The LORD is my portion,' says my soul, 'therefore I have hope in Him.' The LORD is good to those who wait for Him, to the person who seeks Him." (Lamentations 3: 22-25)

I've always liked the little poem Corrie ten Boom famously composed:

If you look at the world, you'll be distressed.
If you look within, you'll be depressed.
If you look at God, you'll be at rest.[4]

When Jeremiah began to look away from his troubles and locked his gaze again on the Lord, Satan's fake news channel faded away like so much background noise. The prophet realized that God is still good no matter how terrible his circumstances might be.

The New American Standard Bible uses the term "lovingkindnesses" in verse 22. It's not a word you and I toss around much these days, but it remains very descriptive of our Lord. It comes from the Hebrew word *chesed*, which speaks of God's loyal, covenant love. It's used in the Old Testament 183 times. You can count on God's love for you, a love that is rooted in the cross.

Years ago, I heard the late great Henry Blackaby say something along these lines: "The way God shows His love to you and me is *outside* our lives."[5] His love is not tied to the specifics of our daily lives. We tend to think the opposite, of course. We imagine that when God does something good, sweet, or unexpected for us, we will smile and say, "Isn't life wonderful? I'm experiencing God's love." But what if tomorrow is different? What if none of those good, sweet, happy things happen to you tomorrow? What if your tomorrow is terribly difficult or sad or filled with loss? What then? Does that mean He no longer loves you?

Our situations and fortunes in life rise and fall like the tide. You can't evaluate God's love for you based on your circumstances because your circumstances change all the time.

But something real happened in space and time, 2,000 years ago, something that was outside your life, and yet it intimately involves your life.

---

[4]Footnote: Boom, Corrie ten, and John Sherrill. *The Hiding Place: The Triumphant True Story Of Corrie ten Boom*. (Penguin Random House USA, 1984.)
[5]Footnote: Blackaby, Henry. *The Ways Of God: Working Through Us To Reveal Himself To A Watching World*. (Nashville: B & H Pub. Group, 2010.)

Jesus went to the cross for you. With great determination and deliberation, Jesus surrendered His lifeblood for you. Surely, He died for the whole world (1 John 2:2), but specifically, He died for you—little insignificant you, as if you were the only person in the world who needed saving. The Apostle Paul tells us so clearly, "But God demonstrates His own love toward us, in that while we were yet sinners, Christ died for us." (Romans 5:8)

Someone has well said, "I asked Jesus how much He loved me, and He stretched out His arms and died." And he died for you before you were ever born! Listen, there's nothing that you can do to get God to love you anymore, and there's nothing you can do to get God to love you any less. He just loves you! He has chosen to love you. He loves you when you're good, and He loves you when you're bad. He even loves you when your faith fails as Peter's did that unforgettable night when he denied three times that he knew Jesus at all. God loves you! And His love is LOYAL.

When Jeremiah writes, "the LORD's lovingkindnesses indeed never cease," he uses three little Hebrew words, *lo, lo, lo,* which actually means 'no, no, no.' His lovingkindnesses indeed never, never, never cease, and His compassions never fail.

We all hate to overuse or trivialize the word 'awesome.' But here is something absolutely, undeniably awesome. You know all of the qualities of God's love, compassion, and mercy that we've been talking about? Well, check this out: They are NEW every single morning. Every morning, when you open your eyes to greet a new day, there is a fresh, untapped, undiminished, undiluted, immeasurable supply of grace, kindness, and tender compassion. And it is there for you.

When Jeremiah quit listening to the spin doctor and lifted his eyes to heaven, his whole perspective on life changed.

There's nothing that you can do to get God to love you anymore, and there's nothing you can do to get God to love you any less. He just loves you!

Pastor Jeff

Regardless of your circumstances, *God is still good.* In Zephaniah 3:17 the prophet sings,

"The LORD your God is in your midst,
A victorious warrior.
He will exult over you with joy,
He will be quiet in His love,
He will rejoice over you with shouts of joy."

That's God! So, no matter what you're facing in life or how bad the circumstances, God is still good.

You just need to wait for Him, and remember that He doesn't work on your timetable; He works on His timetable. So, wait for Him, and keep seeking Him. As Jeremiah told us (in his better moments), "The LORD is good to those who wait for Him, to the person who seeks Him." And here's something to remember: Waiting is never passive. It isn't counting flowers on the wall and playing solitaire till dawn. Waiting on God is *active.* As I wait for Him, I seek Him with all my heart and soul.

You are no doubt familiar with the name Charles Lindberg, a very famous person in American history. As a daring pilot, one of the things Lindberg did was take on the daunting task of flying the first solo flight from New York to Paris across the Atlantic Ocean in a little plane called *The Spirit of St. Louis.* This was 1927, and no one had ever attempted such a thing or achieved such a distance. The little plane went 100 miles an hour, which meant that the journey would take him 33 and half hours—if he could actually make it.

The plane didn't have any of the sophisticated instruments that even the most basic planes carry today. But Lindbergh had a compass, probably a Thermos of coffee, and a general idea of where he needed to go.

Relatively early in the flight, however, he ran into trouble when the plane entered a bank of storm clouds choked with moisture. When he noticed the condensation on the wings begin to freeze, he knew he was in

Every morning, when you open your eyes to greet a new day, there is a fresh, untapped, undiminished, undiluted, immeasurable supply of grace, kindness, and tender compassion. And it is there for you.

a life-or-death dilemma. Should he turn back and end his quest? What would he do? If he didn't come up with something quickly, the fragile wings would freeze over, and he would end up in the Atlantic.

In the midst of this critical turmoil, Lindbergh had a moment of inspiration. Suddenly pulling back on the stick, he put his little silver monoplane into a steep climb. Up and up he went with the clouds still surrounding him and blinding him. Then, in an instant, he broke through the dark ceiling into dazzling sunshine under a deep vault of faultless blue.

Lindbergh must have smiled at that moment, remembering an old truth he already knew. When you're in the fog, when you're in the storm clouds, if you point your nose skyward, if you keep going up, you will find that the sun is always shining.

We all walk through times of disappointment, heartbreak, and pain. And in those moments, a real devil who really hates you will come to you in the night, and try to spin your circumstances in the worst way. "You can't trust God," he will say. "He doesn't love you. He won't see you through."

In that moment, you need to pull back on the stick of faith and go up, up, up, up until you see the Son in all His radiance and love, until you get your eyes on Him again, the God who loves you, the God who is faithful, the God who is worth it all.

-5-

A Fork in the Road

*"If you don't know where you are going,
you might wind up someplace else."*
—YOGI BERRA

Years ago, I came across the story of a man who set out on a road trip in his trusty pickup truck.

Everything was going well, until he approached a fork in the road. He knew his destination was to the right, but to his consternation, there were a couple of orange cones right in the middle of his intended route, along with a sign that said ROAD CLOSED in big, bold letters. An orange detour marker pointed toward the road on the left.

He looked down the road that was supposedly closed. It looked fine to him. After a minute or so, the driver reasoned, *Why should I go left when I want to go right? I don't want to take some roundabout route that will chew up all kinds of time. Besides, it's way out of my way. It's terribly inconvenient. And I don't see any reason why that road should be closed. Whoever put up that sign probably didn't know what he was talking about.*

With his decision made, the driver carefully drove around the detour sign and the orange cones and went on his way down the right-hand road.

All went well for the next few miles, and the driver smiled at himself, thinking, *I knew it! There was nothing wrong with this road. Me and my pickup, we can get through anything.*

But as it turned out, he couldn't.

As he approached a deep canyon, the hairs on the back of his neck bristled as he realized that there was no bridge over the chasm. Braking to a stop, he hit the steering wheel with his hand. "Crud!" he said. "So *that's* why the road was closed. The bridge is out." Carefully turning around, he drove back the five miles to the fork. When he arrived, he noticed that on the other side of the of the ROAD CLOSED sign, were these mocking words: "WELCOME BACK, STUPID."

We may not like to admit it, but sometimes you and I can be like that cocky driver who thought he knew better than the road signs. When it comes to our own lives, we think we know best. We think that we can make a way where there seems to be no way. And as it happens, we get a lot of encouragement from an evil power beyond ourselves using that same line of thinking.

Where the Road Divides

What do you do when you're in a situation that requires a decision, and you see a sign before you that clearly says "God's Way" and another sign pointing in a different direction that says "My Way"?

It's a fork in the road. You can't go back. You have to decide. In fact, *not* to decide is to decide.

Frank Sinatra famously sang a line in his signature 1969 hit, "I did it my way." But what do you do when there is a clear decision to be made, a choice that really boils down to God's way or your way?

For many people in today's world, that's not even a question. They don't even acknowledge God or His way. They will take their own way and follow their own inclinations every time. In Romans 1:22, the Apostle Paul had a word for such people. He wrote, "Professing to be wise, they became fools." The word for *fools* in this verse is the same word from which we get our English word *moron*. *"Professing themselves to be wise, they became morons."*

They might be very nice morons. They might be mature, refined, and quite sophisticated morons. They might have advanced academic degrees or have attained great status or celebrity. But they are morons just the same. Anyone who deliberately denies the Almighty, scorns His Word, and shuns His ways, claiming to know more than He knows, is a F-O-O-L. As David wrote, "The fool has said in his heart 'There is no God.'" (Psalm 14:1)

Throughout Israel's history in the Old Testament, many in the Jewish nation believed in God; they just didn't want to obey Him or follow His Word. When their rebellious actions inevitably led them into deep trouble, they would blame God for their situation. In Ezekiel 18:25, the Lord speaks to them about their complaints:

> "You say, 'The way of the LORD is not right.' Hear now, O house of Israel! Is My way not right? Is it not your ways that are not right?"

They were saying, in essence, "God, you're bringing judgment into our lives, and it isn't fair. You're not fair! You're not just. You're not doing right, and Your ways aren't right!"

Take note of that little word *ways*. It's used over and over, hundreds of times in the Old Testament. The word means "a road, a path, a direction, a manner, a course, or a moral character." So, when you are using the word in relation to God, you are speaking of the road of God, the path of God, the moral character of God, the direction of God, or the way God does things.

God's people said, "We don't like how He does things. It's not balanced. It's not straight." It's like being at a deli counter where the employee is weighing out some meat for you but has his thumb on the scale. And you say, "That's not right. That's not accurate. You're cheating me."

People say similar things today. They may not verbalize it, but they will say in their hearts, "Forget it! I don't care about the Lord's way. It's

Anyone who deliberately denies the Almighty, scorns His Word, and shuns His ways, claiming to know more than He knows, is a F-O-O-L.

not right for me, and it's not my truth. I'll go where I want to go—I know what's best for me."

In a previous chapter, we looked at the sobering truth contained in Proverbs 14:12: "There is a way which seems right to a man, but its end is the way of death." It might seem right that you can blow past the sign that says, "Bridge Out, Road Closed." It might seem right that you can drive around God's warning cones and detour signs and head in that direction. But eventually, the truth will tell. The bridge is out! A sheer cliff looms ahead. If you keep going that way, you will run out of road because the end of that way is death.

What follows are two truths about the way ahead of each one of us.

First Truth: The Devil Wants You to Think God's Way is All Wrong

"Yet you say, 'The way of the Lord is not right.' Hear now, O house of Israel! Is My way not right? Is it not your ways that are not right?" (Ezekiel 18:25)

The fake news from Satan is that God's way is all wrong. God's exiled people in Ezekiel 18 made that claim, but the whole concept dates back to the beginning of time.

Remember the conversation between Eve and the serpent back in Genesis 3? Let's review it again.

"Now the serpent was more crafty than any beast of the field which the Lord God had made. And he said to the woman, "Indeed, has God said, 'You shall not eat from any tree of the garden'?" The woman said to the serpent, "From the fruit of the trees of the garden we may eat; but from the fruit of the tree which is in the middle of the garden, God has said, 'You shall not eat from it or touch it, or you will die.'" The serpent said to the woman, "You surely will not die! For God knows that in the day you eat from it your eyes will be opened, and you will be like God, knowing good and evil."

—Genesis 3:1-5

So, right from the beginning, the devil launched his fake news channel. And in his very first recorded broadcast, he said, "Hey Eve, you don't want to go God's way. You can't trust Him! He's *lying* to you. Is God really telling you that you'll die if you eat that fruit? No way! You won't—and God knows it! There are no consequences for disobeying God. And let me explain something else to you. God is actually holding out on you! Sure, there are plenty of good trees around and lots of good fruit to eat. But this tree is special. God has kept you from the best. If you eat from this tree, you will actually be like God, knowing good and evil. You think God wants your best? He doesn't!"

So, here is Satan's lie: *God's way is restrictive. God's way is dated. God's way is unfair. And what's more, God's way is just plain BORING.* The devil's fake news is all calculated to slam the character and nature of God, and it started almost before the paint was fully dry on this brand-new planet.

To this very moment, Satan is using the same old tired lines. His fake news is really a very, very old false story. But since it keeps on working, he keeps on using it: "This Christianity thing is like wearing chains! Do you really want to be a monk locked in a cell somewhere? Are you kidding me? God is so restrictive. People who believe the Bible—that old, ancient Book—are really trying to hem you in and keep you from enjoying and experiencing life. Wake up, this is the twenty-first century!"

Here is Satan's lie: God's way is restrictive.

God's way is dated. God's way is unfair.

And what's more, God's way is just plain BORING.

I remember talking to a guy about the Lord when I was in college. He was in a fraternity and was big on the campus party scene. I was speaking to him about a relationship with God through His Son Jesus. But this guy didn't have a relationship with God, and he didn't want one. As I reasoned with him, I knew what he was thinking without a word coming out of his mouth. In fact, it was written all over his face.

Seriously? You're talking to me about giving my life to Jesus? That would be the same thing as saying, "No more fun, no more pleasure, no more excitement." If I gave my life to Jesus, I'd have to come to your stupid campus Bible studies, sit around a circle with a bunch of losers, and sing Kumbaya. Well, who wants to do that? Definitely not me! I mean, what does Billy Joel say? "I'd rather laugh with the sinners than cry with the saints. Sinners are much more fun."

So, the fake news has been out there a long, long time that the devil's way is fun and exciting, while God's way is stiff, stodgy, and boring—a real yawner.

But guess what? It's a flat-out lie, and it has always been a lie.

Jesus said, "The thief comes only to steal and kill and destroy; I came that they may have life, and have *it* abundantly." (John 10:10)

Why did people come by the thousands to catch a glimpse of Jesus and hear Him teach? Why did people search for Him and seek Him from early in the morning until late at night? Why did little kids line up to sit in His lap? Why did the temple cops sent by the religious leaders to arrest Jesus come back empty-handed? Shaking their amazed heads, they told their leaders, "Never has a man spoken the way this man speaks." (John 7:46)

Why were men, women, and children so incredibly attracted to Jesus? Maybe John said it best: "And the Word became flesh, and dwelt among us, and we saw His glory, glory as of the only begotten from the Father, full of grace and truth" (John 1:14). Everywhere Jesus went, the people were saying, "We've never heard anyone talk like this! We've never seen anyone like this!" And when He finally peeled back the veil of His humanity on the Mount of Transfiguration, Peter, James, and John got a glimpse of His glory. They were awestruck as His face began to shine like the sun and His garments began to radiate the brightest white.

What does all of this tell us? The Lord of all creation is not boring. In fact, He is the furthest thing from boring that there is. But this lie has been the devil's line of attack from the dawn of civilization. And after he's pushed that "boring" lie for a while, he will often come back and say, "God says that certain pleasures in life are forbidden. He just wants you to live like a lonely hermit! I see it like this: If it looks good, tastes good, and feels good, it IS good." As the old Debby Boone song states, "It can't be wrong, if it feels so right!"[1]

Back in Genesis 3, in the Garden of Eden, Satan led Eve to begin fixating on the one tree in that whole vast and beautiful garden that was forbidden. She started saying to herself, *This tree is really beautiful. The fruit looks wonderful. What's the problem with it? Why in the world has God forbidden it?* Once the devil gets you to start fixating on the forbidden, he's got you in his grasp.

As Eve began to stare at the forbidden fruit, her heart began to race with anticipation. She could just imagine how good it was going to taste and how wonderful it was going to be to have her eyes opened, whatever that might mean. She unhooked the fruit from its stem, and took a bite. It was delicious! It was exhilarating! She gave some to Adam, who was with her, and he ate. They were now in this forbidden fruit thing together!

---

[1]Footnote: Debby Boone, "You Light Up My Life," recorded 1977, [track number] on You Light Up My Life, Columbia Records, [access type].

The fact is sin's pleasures are mostly front-loaded. The thrill and good vibes are on the front end, and all the misery, regret, and consequences are on the back end.

Pastor Jeff

Although the Bible doesn't say that the forbidden fruit was delicious, we can safely surmise that it was. You see, sin does taste good initially. There's pleasure in sin, but the Bible tells us it's a passing pleasure. In Hebrews 11:25, we read that Moses chose "to endure ill-treatment with the people of God (rather) than to enjoy the passing pleasures of sin."

The fact is sin's pleasures are mostly front-loaded. The thrill and good vibes are on the front end, and all the misery, regret, and consequences are on the back end. Remember the story of the prodigal son? When he pocketed his father's inheritance, took off on his own, and blew the whole thing on parties and prostitutes, he was having fun and singing, "Let the good times roll." But then the money ran out, his friends bailed out, and a famine hit. He ended up with nothing. The only job he could find was feeding the pigs. He was a Jew feeding unclean swine. Can it get any worse? Yes, it can. In his intense hunger, he was longing to eat the pig slop. The pleasures of his sin had turned to pain and devastation, as they always do.

That's the way it is with sin. If you blow past the ROAD CLOSED sign, you can enjoy a short season of sunshine and rainbows. But eventually you will come to the reality that the bridge is out. Then you are in serious trouble with nowhere to go.

Second Truth: The Lord Wants You to Know that His Way is Always Right

Many of us these days have come to depend on smartphones with GPS capabilities.

You won't catch me saying anything negative about GPS. I love it. It's been such a Godsend for me because I am directionally challenged at the best of times. If I come to a T in the road, which way should I go? Right? Left? Turn back? Flip a coin? I can't seem to get it right—and my daughter Amy is just like me. My wife Debbie advises us, "Just go the opposite direction from the way you *think* you should go." Amy recently told her mom,

We're all directionally challenged

when it comes to life. We need the

Word of God and the Spirit of God to

guide us and keep us on course.

Pastor Jeff

"You know, that's good advice. If I choose against my natural instincts, I end up going in the right direction!"

While I admit to having a defective inner compass, we're all directionally challenged when it comes to life. We need the Word of God and the Spirit of God to guide us and keep us on course.

I love the passage in Isaiah that speaks of the Lord as the Teacher who guides us. The prophet writes: "He, your Teacher will no longer hide Himself, but your eyes will behold your Teacher. Your ears will hear a word behind you, 'This is the way, walk in it,' whenever you turn to the right or to the left." (Isaiah 30:20-21)

God does this every day of our lives through His Spirit and through His Word. And He wants us to know—deep down in our souls—that His way is always right.

In Psalm 19:7-9, David writes,

"The law of the LORD is perfect, restoring the soul;
The testimony of the LORD is sure, making wise the simple.
The precepts of the LORD are right, rejoicing the heart;
The commandment of the LORD is pure, enlightening the eyes.
The fear of the LORD is clean, enduring forever;
The judgments of the LORD are true; they are righteous
altogether."

Do you want to be happy and have a life that's worth living? Do what the Lord says. Follow His Word and His ways. Let His Holy Spirit fill you and guide you. Why? Because His laws are good. In fact, they are always right. Mark it down: You are blessed and happy when you stop *debating* and start *obeying*.

So many people waste precious time and miss priceless opportunities in life because they debate in their hearts about whether to follow God's way or not. As they hit the fork in the road, they say, "I should probably go to the left. I think that's what God wants me to do. But maybe in this instance, maybe this time, He would be okay if I went the other way." And they deliberate and argue in their hearts whether the Word of God is right or not.

Have you ever been praying or spending some time with the Lord when you hear that "still, small voice" whispering to you about something? Maybe He is saying, *You were unkind to your wife today. You need to talk to her and ask her to forgive you.* But you don't really want to confess that sin to your wife—for all kinds of reasons (but mostly pride). So you tell the Lord you will think about it, or maybe do it later.

Do you want to know where happiness awaits?

I'll tell you exactly where it awaits.

In Psalm 119:47-48a, the psalmist writes: "I shall delight in Your commandments, which I love. And I shall lift up my hands to Your commandments, which I love."

In the Old Testament, you lifted up your hands when you wanted to pray to the Lord and praise Him. Solomon, in his great prayer of dedication for the new temple in Jerusalem, "spread out his hands toward heaven." It was common to pray with uplifted hands.

But lifting your hands also means something else, doesn't it? It's the universal sign for *surrender*. When you lift your hands to God, whether you are praying or praising Him in a worship service, you are saying, "I surrender, Lord. I yield to Your commands. I place my life in Your hands. I acknowledge that Your voice is right, and Your way is right."

When you do that and surrender to God's way, you are on the road to happiness. It may not be easy. It may go cross-grain to contemporary culture. It may be the very opposite of what your flesh wants you to do. Satan and his demons may be pushing the other way with all their might.

But God's ways are always right. Always.

Let's take a quick look at a few of our culture's most divisive issues and what God has to say about them.

What God says about sexual immorality is right

Think about sexual immorality in our country. It is rampant. Fornication (having sex before you are married) and adultery (having sex outside your marriage) are seemingly no longer considered sinful. One night stands are the order of the day. What does God have to say about this subject? In Hebrews 13:4 we read, "Marriage is to be held in honor among all, and the marriage bed is to be undefiled; for fornicators and adulterers God will judge." Sex outside of marriage is wrong. Adultery is wrong. Homosexuality is wrong. It doesn't matter what the magazines or movies or websites or late-night talk show hosts say. These actions are sinful and wrong. The price for living a life of sexual immorality and sexual perversion is extremely high. Listen to the Apostle Paul:

> "Or do you not know that the unrighteous will not inherit the kingdom of God? Do not be deceived; neither fornicators, nor idolaters, nor adulterers, nor effeminate, nor homosexuals, nor thieves, nor *the* covetous, nor drunkards, nor revilers, nor swindlers, will inherit the kingdom of God."
>
> —1 Corinthians 6:9-10

When you read that list, you might find yourself saying, "Well, man, that nails me to the wall." But guess what? It nailed some of those Corinthians to the wall, too. Some were living together outside of marriage, some were practicing homosexuals, some were idolaters, and some were thieves.

But Paul goes on to say this:

> "Such were some of you; but you were washed, but you were sanctified, but you were justified in the name of the Lord Jesus Christ and in the Spirit of our God."
>
> —1 Corinthians 6:11

Regardless of our past, when we call

on the name of the Lord Jesus,

He cleanses us, makes us holy, and

makes us right with God!

Pastor Jeff

Thank God! Regardless of our past, when we call on the name of the Lord Jesus, He cleanses us, makes us holy, and makes us right with God!

He is a God who forgives, but His standards concerning sexual immorality are right—and those standards haven't moderated or "evolved" since the first century. So, when you watch sitcoms and movies on TV, and hear about stuff people do at school or at work, don't say to yourself, "Well, everybody's progressed concerning morality, so it must be okay." It's not okay. It's not okay because the Judge of all the earth tells you what is right and what is wrong. And if you try to drive around those orange cones and ignore the big sign that says, ROAD CLOSED, you will drive off a cliff. The road of sexual immorality will lead to destruction.

What God says about gender identity is right

In the gospel of Matthew, Jesus quoted these words from the book of Genesis:

> "... Have you not read that He who created them from the beginning MADE THEM MALE AND FEMALE, and said, 'FOR THIS REASON A MAN SHALL LEAVE HIS FATHER AND MOTHER AND BE JOINED TO HIS WIFE, AND THE TWO SHALL BECOME ONE FLESH'?"

> —Matthew 19:4-5

What is marriage, according to Jesus? It's a male coming together with a female, and the two becoming one flesh. Marriage is between a man and a woman. God made two (and only two) genders: male and female. Two sexes and two genders. If you are struggling with your gender, let me give you a little insight. *Your sex IS your gender!* It's not complicated. If you were born with an XX chromosome, you're a female; if you were born with an XY chromosome, you're a male.

Yes, there is certainly a condition called gender dysphoria. It's the distress a person experiences as a result of a conflict between his or her sex and gender. Such an individual might say, "Well, I know I'm a biological male, but I identify with females. And I'm so torn because my body tells me one thing and my mind tells me another."

Do you want to know how to silence the inner conflict and turmoil? In the spirit of Psalm 119:48, you can lift up your hands to God's commandments and say, "Lord, You are my creator. You made me to be who you want me to be. You do not make mistakes. You did not put me in the wrong body, even though it feels like it to me. God, I am dealing with a host of emotions and thoughts. Help me to believe the obvious truth that my gender is inseparably linked to my biological sex. Help me to put this struggle to bed as I choose your truth over my feelings. In Jesus' name, amen."

In the strongest terms possible, today's contemporary culture denies these most basic of truths. Some misinformed Christians, in the name of compassion, might say, "Being homosexual or transgender isn't right for me, but maybe it's okay for you." No. That isn't an option. If God, in His Word, says the road is closed, then the road is closed. No matter what anyone may tell you, God's closed road signs are there for a reason. Those roads lead to death.

In a 2016 Johns Hopkins study of gender and sexuality, two psychiatrists, Paul McHugh and Lawrence Meyer, concluded: "There is absolutely zero evidence that anyone is born homosexual." And concerning transgenderism, they said, "If you go down that road, you are 19 times more likely to die by suicide."[2]

Why the unhappiness? Why the higher suicide rate for these poor souls? It is because you can't live in fundamental rebellion against God without there being serious mental, emotional, and spiritual consequences. You can't tell the God of the universe that He dropped the ball concerning

---

[2]Footnote: L. S. Mayer and P. R. McHugh. "Sexuality and Gender." The New Atlantis, No. 50, Fall 2016.. Accessed 15 September 2024. https://www.thenewatlantis.com/publications/Executive Summary – Sexuality and Gender.

your creation, and now you are going to have to right (through mutilation surgeries and puberty blockers) what He has wronged. Anyone who assumes this posture is going to find themselves in freefall mode. The end results of this upside-down thinking are devastating for all involved. Based on the statistics, the misery index soars and suicide often ensues.

What God says about the sanctity of life is right

If you keep up with the news in our country, this is the big issue. With every election cycle, the debate seems to grow sharper, deeper, and more acrimonious. One side speaks about a baby's "right to life," and the other side goes on and on about "a woman's right to choose."

"My body, my choice," is the cry of pro-abortion women. That sounds good and right until you understand that the baby growing inside the mother is another body entirely! Your baby is not your body. You have no right to choose to kill that body, just as you have no right to murder anyone. The sixth commandment is crystal clear: "You shall not murder" (Exodus 20:13). Make no mistake, abortion is murder according to the Word of God. It is the taking of innocent life.

In Psalm 139:13-14, David writes: "For You formed my inward parts; You wove me in my mother's womb. I will give thanks to You, for I am fearfully and wonderfully made. Wonderful are Your works, and my soul knows it very well."

In the book of Jeremiah, the Lord tells the young prophet, "Before I formed you in the womb I knew you, And before you were born I consecrated you; I have appointed you a prophet to the nations." (Jeremiah 1:5)

Do you know who is into abortion up to his eyeballs? Do you know who concerns himself with killing babies? The devil! You can see it again and again in Scripture. He started with Pharaoh back in the book of Exodus, who wanted to kill all the boy babies born to Hebrew families. His solution? Throw them into the Nile as soon as they were born. Feed them to the crocodiles! And in the years to come, what did they do in Israel when they began

The things that are right are right because they come from a Holy God. They align with His nature. And by the same token, things that don't align with His nature are wrong.

to worship the false gods Chemosh, Molech, and the gods of the Canaan-ites? They would take their babies and offer them as a sacrifice in the fire. What happened in the New Testament with King Herod when Jesus was born in Bethlehem? "Then when Herod saw that he had been tricked by the magi, he became very enraged, and sent and slew all the male children who were in Bethlehem and all its vicinity, from two years old and under, accord-ing to the time which he had determined from the magi." (Matthew 2:16)

God says that human life is sacred. John the Baptist had been six months in his mother Elizabeth's womb when Mary, the mother of Jesus, came to visit her. Do you remember what happened when Mary entered the room? The little baby leaped for joy in Elizabeth's womb. He was already becoming who he would be. God was forming him and knitting him together. Before he was ever conceived, the angel Gabriel told Zechariah that the baby would be "filled with the Holy Spirit while yet in his mother's womb." (Luke 1:15)

He was a person.

When does life begin? It clearly begins at conception. And anyone who says, "I'm a Bible-believing Christian, and I am for abortion," is either a liar or a greatly deceived believer. Taking the life of an unborn child goes directly against Scripture and the heart of God. He is the giver of life and the Lord of life! As far as God is concerned, every life is planned.

In 2024, liberal talk show host Bill Maher said the quiet part out loud. The subject he and his guests were discussing was abortion. Maher said, "I can respect the absolutist position. I really can. I scold the left when they say, 'Oh, you know what, they just hate women, people who aren't pro-choice.' They don't hate women. They just made that up. They think it's murder, and it kind of is. I'm just okay with that, I am. I mean, there are eight billion people in the world. I'm sorry, we won't miss you. That's my position on it."

While we recoil in shock at his gruesome and calloused position on the issue, we can surely appreciate his honesty. Abortion is murder, brutal murder by dismemberment of the innocent unborn. And it is a heinous sin against God that will bring certain judgment.

What God says about ANYTHING is right

Going back to that amazing, multi-dimensional chapter in Scripture, it says in Psalm 119:128: "Therefore I esteem right all *Your* precepts concerning everything, I hate every false way."

That about covers it, doesn't it? *I believe ALL Your ways are right about EVERYTHING.* Why? Because You are God! Because You are Creator. Because you are Judge of all the earth.

The things that are right are right because they come from a Holy God. They align with His nature. And by the same token, things that don't align with His nature are wrong.

Maybe you agree with the psalmist concerning God that "all Your ways are right about everything." That's good. That means you've taken the right fork in the road. But it doesn't mean that you won't continue to struggle with sin. Of course you will. We all do. You may have great difficulty with sexual temptations. You may have to fight an ongoing battle with lust, pornography, fornication, adultery, or even homosexuality. You might feel that pull every day. The fact is, I don't know very many men who don't struggle from one degree to another with the issue of sexual lust. We all struggle with temptation. We all experience failure at times. The Apostle John tells us, "If we say that we have no sin, we are deceiving ourselves and the truth is not in us." (1 John 1:8)

When God declares a road closed,

He has very good reasons for doing so.

Struggling with sin isn't the problem—as long as we acknowledge that our sin *is* sin. The danger comes when we stop calling it sin. Tired of the struggle, someone might say, "Well, I keep doing this again and again, so I'm just going to accept it in my life and forget what God says about it." No! That's not the answer. The answer is to lift up your hands to the commandments you love and say, "God, I admit and acknowledge that Your way is right. I'm having difficulty with this particular area of my life, but I want to stay on Your road. Give me strength to do the right thing."

We are blessed—every one of us—when we stop debating and start obeying. When God declares a road closed, He has very good reasons for doing so.

-6-

Victory or Defeat

"Wretched man that I am! Who will set me free from the body of this death? Thanks be to God through Jesus Christ our Lord! So then, on the one hand I myself with my mind am serving the law of God, but on the other, with my flesh the law of sin."

—ROMANS 7:24-25

Does the name Vinko Bogataj ring a bell?

Maybe not. But countless sports fans of a certain age have no doubt seen him scores of times on TV without ever learning his name.

Vinko Bogataj was a Yugoslavian ski jumper from years ago. Actually, ski *flier* is probably a more apt description. These are the guys that rocket down a steep slope, lean forward over their skis, and go sailing off into the wild blue yonder, traveling hundreds of feet through the air before making a graceful landing.

Or at least, that's how it's *supposed* to work.

In the 1970 World Ski Flying Championships in Oberstdorf, West Germany, the 22-year-old Bogataj was competing for Yugoslavia. The weather was particularly nasty at those games, with more wind, ice, and snow than many of the participants had bargained for. ABC's Wide World of Sports, that iconic sports program that ran from the 60s through the 90s, was on the scene covering the ski jumps when young Bogataj prepared to take his final turn at the top of the slope.

As Bogataj launched into his jump, the announcer was saying, "The youngster, he's inexperienced. He fell on his first jump. A lot of speed on that . . . ."

But then something went wrong. The announcer started shouting, "Look out! Look at him go! Oh, oh, baby! What a terrible fall!"

In later years, Bogataj's daughter Sandy described her dad's situation at that moment. "It was bad weather, and he had to wait around 20 minutes before he got permission to start. He remembers that he couldn't see very well. The track was in bad shape, and just before he could jump, the snow or something grabbed his skis, and he fell. From that moment, he doesn't remember anything."[1]

It's probably merciful that he couldn't remember. Because instead of sailing gracefully off the in-run in the classic forward-leaning position, the young athlete tumbled off the jump head over heels—arms and legs flailing, bouncing down the course before crashing through a retaining fence near a crowd of spectators. Most onlookers feared he was dead. For all the drama, however, Bogataj's only injuries were a mild concussion and a broken ankle.

When the ABC sports executives saw the footage of that spectacular fall, they immediately knew what they wanted for the Wide World of Sports's opening scene for their weekly program. If you were a sports fan in that era, you will remember how the program began each week, with the words, "Spanning the globe to bring you the constant variety of sports. The thrill of victory . . . and the agony of defeat." Vinko Bogataj's disaster, of course, was the perfect backdrop for "the agony of defeat."

---

[1] Footnote: T. Neumann. "Whatever Happened to the 'Agony of Defeat' Ski Jumper?' ESPN. com, accessed 15 September 2024. https://www.espn.com/olympics/story/_/id/17310907/ happened-agony-defeat-ski-jumper.

For decades afterward, sports fans watched the young Yugoslav's unhappy moment, week after week, over and over again. Vinko Bogataj became an American icon for a crushing defeat.

(By the way, the man has gone on to live a happy life with a wife and two daughters in Slovenia. Setting aside his skis, he picked up a paintbrush and became an excellent landscape painter.)

ABC Sports could have used many different film clips to illustrate "the thrill of victory" but not so much the "agony of defeat." We all remember moments when—as participants or spectators—we saw our favorite team score the winning basket, goal, homerun, or touchdown. We love the thrill of victory. And we have all suffered through the agony of seeing our favorite sports team go down in defeat.

But those two words, victory and defeat, go far beyond sports, don't they? When it comes to your life, your Christian life, what do you experience the most? Are there more spiritual victories or more spiritual defeats?

When I was in college, a man named David Ferguson taught our college department at church. To this day, I remember what he told us about defeats in our spiritual life. His words went something like this:

"Some of you," he said, "have a sin that just plagues you. It's like a shadow. It dogs your steps, and you can't seem to shake it. It's almost like there's a handle on your back. And just when you think you're starting to take off spiritually and make some progress in your walk with the Lord, the devil grabs that handle and pulls you down."

We all have different "handles" don't we? In Ephesians 4:27, Paul tells us not to give the devil an "opportunity" or "place" or "foothold" in our lives. We can easily think about this "place" as a "handle." It's the sin you fall prey to over and over and over again. Maybe it's drugs. Maybe it's alcohol. Maybe it's pornography. Maybe it's gossip. Maybe it's insecurity. Maybe it's worry. Maybe it's gluttony. Most likely, you have some sin in your life that keeps rearing its ugly head, eating your lunch and sending you tumbling down the mountain.

He wants you to have a genuine relationship

with Him, experience true salvation, and

walk with Him through all the ups and downs

and highs and lows of life.

Anglican hymn writer William Cowper (1731-1800) wrote a song published in 1772 called, "Oh! For a Closer Walk with God." One of the lyrics is priceless and has become a frequent prayer of my heart:

The dearest idol I have known, whate'er that idol be,
help me tear it from Thy throne and worship only Thee.[2]

In all our lives, we have certain failures that become, as Hebrews 12:1 puts it, "the sin which so easily entangles us." The Modern King James Version calls it "the sin which so easily besets us." Do you have a besetting sin—or several? Besetting sins are the thoughts, activities, or inclinations that we keep tripping over time and time again. These sins seem to defeat us so often that we begin to wonder, *Is victory even possible? If so, why can I not seem to get past this recurring sin?*

So, here is our question: How can you live a life of spiritual victory instead of spiritual defeat? How can you keep from falling head over heels off the end of the ski jump? (Again, and again, and again.) In brief, here's the answer: By recognizing the *lies of the devil* and applying *the truth of God*.

I like to return to Jesus's words on what it means to be a true disciple and walk in spiritual victory. One of my favorite go-to passages is John 8. Right in the middle of an intense—you might say heated—discussion with

---

[2]Footnote: William Cowper. "Oh! For a Closer Walk with God." Olney Hymns, 1772.

the Jewish religious leaders, Jesus says something very pointed and profound about what it means to be set free from the destructive power of sin.

In the pages of this chapter, I would like to highlight two strong directional signals in our Lord's words that point us toward more consistent spiritual victory in our lives.

First Directional Signal: The Lord Wants You to Have Eternal Victory in Heaven

The Lord Jesus wants you to enter into His victory, a mighty triumph that lasts through all the years of your life, whether they be many or few, and continues into eternity. He wants you to have a genuine relationship with Him, experience true salvation, and walk with Him through all the ups and downs and highs and lows of life.

In John 8:31-32 we read:

So Jesus was saying to those Jews who had believed Him, "If you continue in My word, then you are truly disciples of Mine; and you will know the truth, and the truth will make you free."

Were the "Jews who had believed in Him" saved? Was Jesus addressing true, born-again disciples in John 8:31-32? I don't think He was. I think the bulk of these people were just like the folks in John 2:23-24: "Now when He was in Jerusalem at the Passover, during the feast, many believed in His name, observing His signs which He was doing. But Jesus, on His part, was not entrusting Himself to them, for He knew all men."

In other words, many of the Jews who were in Jerusalem for the feast were wowed by His miracles. They followed Him *en masse* because it was the town's biggest, most exciting show. He fed them, He healed the sick, and He raised the dead, so they were very curious. But Jesus knew their hearts inside and out. He knew the real motives of the people who had begun to follow Him.

> *A true disciple is one who comes to Jesus on Jesus' terms. He comes the Lord's way; he doesn't try to come his own way.*

That's why He said, "If you continue in My word, then you are truly disciples of Mine." In other words, *If you want to be a true disciple, here is what you need to do.*

In that day, just as it is today, there were true disciples as well as false ones. But God always desires truth—right down to the core of our being (see Psalm 51:6). So, what is a true disciple? A true disciple is one who *comes to Jesus on Jesus' terms*. He comes the Lord's way; he doesn't try to come his own way.

So then, what is the Lord's way?

In the Lord's Sermon on the Mount, He began with these words: "Blessed are the poor in spirit, for theirs is the Kingdom of heaven" (Matthew 5:3). The poor in spirit, then, are the ones who get to go to heaven. So, the question naturally comes to mind: What does it mean to be poor in spirit? I want to be poor in spirit because Jesus said these people are blessed and will inherit heaven. So, sign me up. But how do I do it?

I believe being poor in spirit means understanding three essentials.

First: You understand that you are totally and completely bankrupt before God.

There's nothing that you look back on in your life and say, "Well, I really accomplished something back then. I must have scored some major points with God on that day." No! Being "poor in spirit" means you don't commend yourself to God. You don't get the prideful idea that you are something truly special. You don't keep a record of your good deeds, kind words, or personal sacrifices. You realize that there is nothing in you that would garner favor with God. You are a bankrupt sinner before the thrice Holy God of the universe.

Second: You understand that there is nothing you can do to change your bankruptcy before God.

There's nothing you can do to save yourself. There's nothing you can do to earn brownie points toward heaven.

Nothing. Zero. Nada.

As the little couplet from the hymn "Rock of Ages" so poignantly states, "Nothing in my hand I bring, simply to Thy cross I cling."[3] In other words, "Lord, I don't have anything to say for myself, and I don't have anything to show. I come empty-handed before You, seeking Your grace and mercy because I have no way to save myself."

Third: You understand that Jesus is the only way, and the great I AM— God in the flesh.

In John 8:58, Jesus told the people, "Truly, truly, I say to you, before Abraham was born, I am." And the people gasped! I AM is the holy name of God. *How dare you blaspheme!* And they picked up stones to stone Him for the sin of blasphemy. But Jesus did not blaspheme—because He is the great I AM! He is God's only Son and man's only Savior. No one will ever get to heaven apart from believing in Jesus and surrendering to Him. When you are poor in spirit, you understand this essential truth.

And that is how anyone comes to salvation in Jesus. It is on His terms, not ours. You come to the Lord on His terms. We come in humility, repentance, and faith . . . or we don't come at all.

Now, the Pharisees and religious leaders in Jesus' day didn't want to come His way. They wanted to come their own way. They had hijacked the

---

[3]Footnote: Augustus Montague Toplady. "Rock of Ages." Hymns, 1776.

Old Testament teachings, creating an elaborate system of laws and rules and a works salvation that God never intended. They ran around with their clipboards and sharp pencils, making sure people checked all the thousands of boxes they had to check if they wanted to be righteous before God. But it was all outward and external. These meticulous rule keepers were nothing more than whitewashed tombs. They looked good on the outside, but the inside was rotten to the core.

These guys weren't poor in spirit; they were proud in spirit. They "trusted in themselves that they were righteous, and viewed others with contempt." (Luke 18:9)

That wicked, self-righteous sentiment is very similar to what the Scripture says about a man named Cain from Genesis chapter 4. Cain, the firstborn son of Adam and Eve, was a farmer. When the time came to offer a sacrifice to God, he came with what he could produce as a farmer: the fruit of the ground. In essence, he was offering the Lord his good works as his sacrifice. "Here, Lord, this is what I am offering to you, from the sweat of my brow and the labor of my hands."

We don't have the full story in Genesis, but it's apparent that Cain wasn't approaching God the way God had told him to—with a blood sacrifice. (Hebrews 9:22 tells us, "Without shedding of blood there is no forgiveness.") In the pride of his heart, Cain wanted to come his own way, offering the best of what he could produce.

What's the evidence that he knew God's way but didn't want to follow it? The evidence is found in Hebrews 11:4, "By faith Abel offered to God a better sacrifice than Cain." Abel, Cain's younger brother, came with a blood sacrifice (see Genesis 4:4). And he brought it by faith. Romans 10:17 tells us, "So then faith comes by hearing, and hearing by the word of God" (NKJV). Faith is a response to revelation. There can be no faith without the Word of God. Abel brought a blood sacrifice because the word of God instructed him to do so. And his faith offering was received.

The Lord had no regard for Cain and his offering because Cain came his own way. Cain came before the Lord on his own terms. He offered to God the fruit of the cursed ground. He offered the very best his hands could produce. It was a works offering and not a faith offering. And God did not want it.

There is an interesting postscript on this incident in Jude, the second-to-last book of the Bible. In Jude 1:11, we read: "Woe to them! For they have gone the way of Cain."

The way of Cain is the way of works. And it is the way of woe. It's coming to God on your own terms. It's the way that leads to death and spiritual defeat forever and ever. The Lord doesn't want that! He wants you to have eternal victory in heaven. A true disciple is the one who comes to Jesus on the Lord's terms.

That's the first truth, and there is no way to express how important it is in print. Why? Because Satan has spread his fake news all over the world, and many people have believed the lies. People still believe they can come to God on their own terms. They imagine that if they attend church, get baptized, serve on a committee or two, put some money in the collection plate, try to be a good person, and not hurt anybody, then they will be right with God. Those things are wonderful, but none of them will get you into heaven. You must come the Lord's way, poor in spirit, understanding you are bankrupt, and that you can't do one single, solitary thing to save yourself.

Jesus, the great I AM, is the only one who can save you.

And He will! But you have to come on His terms.

Second Directional Signal: The Lord Wants You to Have Daily Victory on Earth

This is a "rubber-meets-the-road" moment for Christians.

Someone will say, "I've put my faith and trust in Jesus, and there has been a change in my heart. I do believe I am a true disciple and not a false

No matter who you are (or think you are), you never get beyond the presence and the pull of sin.

disciple, but I'm still struggling with sin. I don't get it, and I don't understand it! The Bible says that if the Son has set me free, then I'm free indeed. I believe that, and yet . . . I'm really struggling."

Let's go back for another look at our Lord's words in John 8:31-32.

"So Jesus was saying to those Jews who had believed Him [those who were checking Him out, those who were seeking, those who were moving closer to Him], 'If you continue in My word, then you are truly disciples of Mine; and you will know the truth, and the truth will make you free.'"

Every true disciple has eternal victory because they've passed out of death into life and have had their names inscribed in the Lamb's Book of Life. I believe the Bible teaches that they will never lose that unspeakably wonderful gift of eternal life. But in addition to that eternal victory, they can also walk in *daily* victory.

In Romans chapter 6, Paul tells us that all those in Christ have been set free from sin. We are "dead to sin, but alive to God in Christ Jesus" (Romans 6:11). Hallelujah! How cool is that!?

But some of us might reply: "Okay, that's what it says on paper, and I will gladly run those words up a flagpole and salute. But how does that truth work itself out in *practice*? I mean, I sure don't *feel* like I'm dead to sin. I'm tempted all the time. So, how can I live dead to sin and alive to God?"

Believe it or not, that on-going struggle is true for every Christian. No matter who you are (or think you are), you never get beyond the *presence and the pull of sin*. On the other side of eternity, when we are in God's presence, we'll finally be free from the struggle with our flesh (our fallen sinful Adamic nature that is against God). In heaven, the presence of and struggle with sin will be banished forever. But that is not true for here and now! We still live with the gravitational pull of sin on this broken planet, and the father of lies is still broadcasting his fake news across all bandwidths.

People in church used to sing about the "sweet by and by," but even they had to deal with the nasty now-and-now. How do we live in such a way that we have victory over those inevitable temptations? How do we live like victory is not just a promise on paper but a living reality infused into our daily lives?

It's important to remember that the same Apostle Paul, who told us in Romans 6 that every believer is dead to sin, also wrote *this* in the very next chapter:

> "For I know that nothing good dwells in me, that is, in my flesh; for the willing is present in me, but the doing of the good *is* not. For the good that I want, I do not do, but I practice the very evil that I do not want. But if I am doing the very thing I do not want, I am no longer the one doing it, but sin which dwells in me."
>
> —Romans 7:18-20

By the way, in Romans 7, Paul is writing as a believer in Jesus. The struggles he felt were not as a lost man, they were as a saved man. Every Christian knows the struggle within. The battle with the flesh is a very real thing. That is why Paul wrote in Galatians 5:16-17, "But I say, walk by the Spirit, and you will not carry out the desire of the flesh. For the flesh sets its desire against the Spirit, and the Spirit against the flesh; for these are in opposition to one another, so that you may not do the things that you please." Paul found victory by walking in the power of the Holy Spirit, and that's how you and I have victory, too.

A true disciple continues day by day in that victory by walking *in the truth*. "You shall know the truth," Jesus said, "and the truth shall make

If you try to coast in the Christian life, you'll never stay in the same spot. You'll always go backward.

you free." You must know the truth and walk in the truth by applying God's truth to your life. And that's the hard part—taking what you know and living it out.

No one said it would be easy! Everything is coming against you as a Christian (and that applies to pastors and Christian authors, too). It's like walking upstream through fast-flowing water: There's a current that pushes us back. If you try to coast in the Christian life, you'll never stay in the same spot. You'll always go backward. Why? Because of the steady, persistent current of evil in our world that gives us constant resistance.

In the face of that, we must keep pushing forward in the truth of God's Word to experience the fullness of the Holy Spirit. In this way, we can enjoy the thrill of victory and not constantly end up in the agony of defeat.

Years ago, I heard a story about a pastor preaching a series of revival meetings in Panama. When he gave the invitation for people to come to the altar and make a decision for Christ, a young woman came forward and said to him, "Pastor, I need you to pray for me. Pray that God would clear out the cobwebs in my life."

And so, he prayed, "God, this woman wants to walk in the light with You. She wants her life to glorify Your Son. Please clear out the cobwebs in her life."

On the second night, when he gave the invitation, the same woman came forward with the same request. "Pastor, I need you to pray for me that God would clear out the cobwebs in my life."

He said, "Well, we prayed for that yesterday."

"I know," she said, "but I just need you to pray that same prayer." So, he prayed again, "God, this woman wants to walk with You. Please clear out the cobwebs in her life."

On the third night of the revival, it happened all over again. The same woman, the same request. But this time, the pastor said, "No! I'm not going to pray that again. We don't need to keep praying for God to clear out the cobwebs in your life. We need to start praying that God will kill the spider!"

In our battle against recurring sins, could it be that we're just brushing away cobwebs? Are we going after the symptoms but missing the source? Why is it that so many Christians are failing miserably in their Christian life? Why are multitudes of believers who are dead to sin seemingly addicted to drugs, alcohol, pornography, bitterness, selfishness, and the like? Are these simply cobwebs—or is it something deeper?

There is a spider of lies that spins the cobweb. And we need to find the spider and put the spider to death. And how do we kill the spider? We kill him with truth.

I want to share with you five truths that are so critical and foundational for us to believe so that we can walk in victory and shield ourselves against Satan's fake news.

Truth #1: God's Love for You is Not Based on Your Performance.

Sometimes, we find ourselves thinking, "God loves me if I'm doing right— if I'm really walking the walk. But when I get off track, when I falter and fail, He doesn't love me."

I call that sort of thinking daisy theology. Do you know about daisy theology?

When I was a kid growing up in our neighborhood, if one of the guys liked a certain girl, he would pick a little flower and begin to pull off the petals, one by one. And with each petal, he would say, "She loves me, she loves me not. She loves me, she loves me not." And all the while, he's hoping that when he gets to the last petal, it will be, "Ah, she loves me!" In a sense, we tend to do that with the Lord. We say, "I'm doing

God loves you because He has chosen to love you, and He loves you with an everlasting love. It doesn't matter how you perform.

good today, I'm walking in victory and sensing God's presence with me; He loves me!" But then, "I really messed up today. I feel totally out of it spiritually; He must not love me right now." *He loves me, He loves me not.* So, we find ourselves living on an emotional roller coaster, never sure whether we're walking in the love of our heavenly Father or not.

That was never how God intended us to live. God loves you because He has *chosen* to love you, and He loves you with an everlasting love. It doesn't matter how you perform; He just loves you. Romans 5:8 tells us, "But God demonstrates His own love toward us, in that while we were yet sinners, Christ died for us."

The lie—the fake news—is that I have to perform well for God to love me. I have to check all the boxes, or He will be disgusted and turn away from me. No! When you live on that kind of performance treadmill, your life will constantly go up and down, and you will find yourself living in a great deal of defeat and discouragement.

Truth #2: God's Acceptance of You is Not Based on Your Performance.

If my mind is in the gutter, if I'm in a fight with my wife, if I fall in this area or that area, I can easily feel that I am outside the circle of His love and favor. I can feel like He doesn't accept me anymore.

Do you know what those feelings are? They are cobwebs. And when you're constantly swatting away cobwebs in any area of your life, you need to find that spider and crush it with the truth. Ephesians 1:6 gives us an amazing truth. Starting in mid-sentence, we read "to the praise of the glory of His grace, by which He made us accepted in the Beloved" (NKJV). We are "accepted in the Beloved," and the Beloved is Jesus Himself. The moment you accept Jesus as Savior and Lord, and God accepts you, you're accepted in the Beloved because you're *in* Christ and God always accepts Christ, and what Christ accomplished on the cross for us.

I have three daughters. I love each of them with all my heart and proudly claim them as my own. When they make good and godly decisions, I am thrilled. But if they make poor, selfish decisions, I am grieved. Yet in my grief, I do not disown them. I don't burn their birth certificate and deny that they were ever mine to begin with. No. Debbie and I love our girls. They are accepted as Schreve girls, not on the basis of worth, but on the basis of birth. And God does the same with His kids. Through my years as a pastor, I've noticed something. If you are an individual who has experienced abuse, abandonment, or rejection in your life, you may have a difficult time believing that God loves you and accepts you for who you are—rather than your performance. In my experience, these people feel diminished and devalued inside.

Have you ever seen a football player make a big play and, in the glory of that moment, act like Superman, pretending to pull open his shirt to reveal a big "S" on his chest? In the jubilation, he's saying, "Hey, do you see that big 'S'? That is there on my chest because I'm Superman!"

But what's going on in the mind of those who have been sexually abused, rejected, or abandoned? They metaphorically pull open their shirt and also reveal a big "S." But the S stands for SHAME. "I'm not Superman. I'm Shameful man because of the things I have done. And how could God want to have a relationship with me? How could He accept me? How could He love me?"

We can easily feel like we are "less than." We can feel like the adulteress Hester Prynne in Nathaniel Hawthorne's classic novel. In our minds, we wear a big scarlet letter everywhere we go, displaying our sin to God and the world. And since we feel like second-class Christians inside, we're going to work and work and work to somehow achieve acceptance with God and others.

People who feel trashy inside tend to do trashy things. Why? Because if I feel like a piece of trash, then it's very easy for me to do trashy things. And the more trashy things you and I do, the more trashy we feel, and the cycle of despair deepens. The devil will say, "Well, that's just who you are, and so it kind of fits together, hand-in-glove."

That's the way it is for so many people. When it comes to a particular habitual sin, they hate it, yet they're drawn to it anyway. And then, when they have stumbled, they hate themselves and say, "No way can God love me. No way can God accept me."

Push away those cobwebs. Take a firm grip on the truth that you are accepted in Christ, you are accepted in the Beloved, and God loves you with an everlasting love—regardless of your performance. Let the truth kill the spider!

Truth #3: God's forgiveness of your sins is complete and total.

The Apostle John writes an encouraging epistle known as First John. In chapter 1, verse 9, we read words that every Christian revisits time and time again. Read this verse aloud, as if you were reading it for the very first time:

> "If we confess our sins, He is faithful and righteous to forgive us our sins and to cleanse us from all unrighteousness."

Take note of the second to the last word.

Do you see it? A-L-L. He forgives us and cleanses us from *all* unrighteousness—not some, not most, but all. Then, in Acts 10:15, we read, "What God has cleansed, no longer consider unholy."

As you consider these important verses, you may be haunted by the ghost of guilt. Maybe the guilt stems from some sinful act you committed last week, last month, last year, five years ago, or even fifty years ago. And if the truth of your heart was fully known, Satan has been using that past sin as a well-worn club to beat you with again and again. Just when you think you are gaining some steam in your walk with Jesus, the devil reminds you of your great sin. Maybe you had an abortion or engaged in an adulterous affair. Maybe you lied and cheated your way to a promotion at work and in the process seriously disparaged a co-worker's reputation. Maybe you bailed out on your family, or shamed your parents, or brought dishonor to the Lord and the ministry through a selfish, sinful act. Over and over, you find yourself beaten down with guilt over that sin or sins from your past. And the evil one whispers, "There's no way God can forgive you for *that evil transgression*. Forget it. You are forever stained with the guilt of that sin."

But his conclusions are a lie! *What we need to do is stop elevating our sin over God's Son.* Our sin, no matter how great, is NEVER greater than the cleansing blood of Jesus Christ. What did the Lord say as He was dying on the cross? "It is finished!" Paid in full! His blood washes whiter than snow. You can walk in forgiveness. I love it in Luke 7:48-50 when Jesus graciously addresses the repentant prostitute weeping at His feet, "Your sins have been forgiven. . . . Your faith has saved you; go in peace." She was not to go away in guilt and shame with a scarlet "A" for her dress. She was to "go in peace" with the knowledge that all her heinous, horrific sins were forgiven and cleansed by the Savior of the world.

Truth #4: God's Will and Ways are Good, and His Grace is Sufficient.

When you go through hard times in life, when the bottom drops out of your world, the devil really moves in with the fake news. He will tell you, "You need to forget this Christianity stuff. You need to forget trusting in God because look where that's gotten you. Nowhere!"

I wrote an article some time ago concerning tragedies in life and how to face a new normal with faith and confidence. A man emailed me in response. This is what he wrote:

What we need to do is stop elevating our sin over God's Son. Our sin, no matter how great, is NEVER greater than the cleansing blood of Jesus Christ.

Pastor Jeff

You want some feedback? How about this: I was blessed financial-ly, and now I am nearly broke. My wife was diagnosed with MS. We were forced to sell our home and move into a smaller one. I was diagnosed with Bells Palsy and hurt my ankle. My mom recently passed away after suffering from dementia. My wife and I had our 38th wedding anniversary yesterday but could not celebrate be-cause her left knee is so swollen that she can hardly walk. I trust Je-sus and ask Him, "Why is it this way? Why all the suffering for my wife and me? Why do we never get a break? Why does it seem like all the evil in the world has taken over? Why doesn't God answer my prayers? I just wish this would all change." God can do it in a blink of an eye, yet He is letting our world go completely insane. Why? Have a nice day, Jeff.

Obviously, he was hurting. He had lots of questions and no answers. He was getting pretty frustrated with God. I get it. Amid the suffering, it's easy to lash out at God and erroneously begin to believe, based on current circumstances, that He isn't good, and His ways aren't right.

When the Apostle Paul was suffering from some really troublesome condition—he called it "a thorn in the flesh"—He prayed three times that the Lord would take it away from him. But the Lord refused. Instead, He gave Paul this tremendous answer to his prayer:

And He has said to me, "My grace is sufficient for you, for power is perfected in weakness." Most gladly, therefore, I will rather boast about my weaknesses, so that the power of Christ may dwell in me. Therefore I am well content with weaknesses, with insults, with distresses, with persecutions, with difficulties, for Christ's sake; for when I am weak, then I am strong.

—2 Corinthians 12:9-10

God is good, God loves you, and His grace is sufficient—enough and more than enough—for your every need.

Pastor Jeff

God has grace for your deepest hurts and challenges in life. No matter what you're going through in life, you must always go back to these unchangeable truths: God is good, God loves you, and His grace is sufficient—enough and more than enough—for your every need. Just keep going God's way, walking God's path, even if you have to limp. Keep waiting for the Lord. As David said, "Wait for the LORD; be strong and let your heart take courage; yes, wait for the LORD." (Psalm 27:14)

Truth #5: God's Spirit Will Never Leave You, and He Will Faithfully Lead You.

Paul said in Galatians 5:16-18: "But I say, walk by the Spirit, and you will not carry out the desire of the flesh. For the flesh sets its desire against the Spirit, and the Spirit against the flesh; for these are in opposition to one another, so that you may not do the things that you please. But if you are led by the Spirit, you are not under the Law."

And here's some great news: We can be led by the Spirit of God!

Pretend like you have never heard those words before in your life. We can be *led*—through life and into eternity—by the Holy Spirit, the third person of the Trinity. Think about it! God Himself living within you, speaking to you, guiding you, warning you, encouraging you. You don't have to fight the battle with sin alone. In fact, you can't! You and I don't have what it takes to live a victorious Christian life. But *He* does!

He is saying to each one of us, "If you will just get out of the way, if you will just yield yourself to Me, then I will live through you. You will be walking by the Spirit and not by the flesh."

The flesh—our old, sinful nature—is pulling and tugging at us, saying, "I want to do this and want to do that. I want to satisfy my base desires!" And the Spirit is saying, "Come soar with Jesus. Keep walking on God's path, and let's live an exciting life of faith and obedience to the will of God."

We really do have a choice. We can discipline our minds in the truth, or we can just kind of float along and get sucked under by Satan's lies and fake news he pumps out on a daily basis.

Aren't you tired of going after cobwebs? Kill the spider with truth!

Make this your prayer today: "Lord, You said in Your Word, 'And you will know the truth, and the truth will make you free.' God, I want to experience this freedom. I want to be free from the devil's handle on my back. I want to be free from falling and falling and falling into the same old sins. God, I want to walk in victory, not defeat. I want what is true on paper to become real in my daily practice of living. You've provided this victory for me. Teach me how to live it. In Jesus' name, amen."

-7-

Disqualified?

"But go, tell His disciples and Peter, 'He is going ahead of you to Galilee; there you will see Him, just as He told you.'"

—MARK 16:7

You may or may not care about golf or golf tournaments.

I get that. Some people can't get enough of golf on TV (me), and many others would rather sit in a room and watch paint dry (my wife, Debbie). Whichever way you lean, however, there are some moments in sports that transcend any particular game or competition and speak to us about our human condition.

That sort of moment occurred in Carnoustie, Scotland, at the 1999 British Open. And the result was an epic, spectacular fail.

The competition between the professional golfers had been going back and forth, but when it came down the stretch one golfer emerged from the pack. It was a young Frenchman named Jean Van de Velde. He was only ranked 153rd in the world, yet he was on the brink of winning the biggest tournament in golf. He had a three shot lead going into the final hole—a 499-yard par four. Everyone watching concluded his victory was in the bag. Who could lose a three shot lead on a par four hole? All he needed was a double bogey to win. Granted, a double bogey is a tall order for a hack like me, but for a pro golfer, it is child's play—or at least it is supposed to be.

Van de Velde didn't win the 1999 British Open. In fact, he ended up in third place. And here's how it happened.

When he stepped to the 18th tee with a three-shot lead, Van de Velde may have been imagining the victory celebration. The coveted Claret Jug trophy would be his! He also may have been thinking about the pride and gratitude of his nation. If he won (and why wouldn't he?), he would be the first French golfer to claim a major tournament title since 1907. Perhaps his concentration was broken. Who knows? At any rate, his rational thinking skills checked out after the 17th hole.

When he stepped to the tee, the Frenchman surprised everyone, including the announcer, by teeing off with a driver. His aggressiveness on this final hole was totally unnecessary. All he had to do was play it safe and win the tournament. His tee shot went wild. It easily could have gone in the water, but he got a lucky bounce that landed him in the short rough. Instead of laying up on his next shot, the smart move, he went for the green with a 2-iron. His errant shot was far right of the hole in the deep weeds. From there, the wheels to his game came flying off. He ended up with a triple bogey. That miserable score landed him in a three-man playoff, a playoff that should have never been. Van de Velde could not overcome the meltdown and took third in a tournament that was undeniably his.

In the golfing world, his defeat is considered the most epic failure in the sport's history. No one comes to the final hole of the British Open with a three-shot lead and *loses*.

But Jean Van de Velde did. And his was a failure of legendary proportions.

In this chapter, we want to discuss another epic failure—one that stands out from all the others and makes an embarrassing defeat at a golf tournament seem like a stroll in the park.

The Wrong Kind of Epic

We're all familiar with personal failures. And anyone who tells you otherwise has just failed the honesty test!

But as we look back on our lives, certain failures rise above others. There are miscues, major blunders, and really bad decisions in your life and mine where we would say, "That's an epic failure!"

What do we do when we experience a huge collapse? As believers, we know that the devil likes to move in on us in moments like that, beat us up with guilt, shame, and condemnation, and try to get us to throw in the towel. That's right in line with what Jesus said about him in John 10:10: "The thief comes only to steal and kill and destroy; I came that they may have life, and have it abundantly."

Sometimes, you will hear testimonies of men and women who have had huge moral failures in their lives before they came to Christ. We rejoice in these personal stories of defeat turned to victory as we think of the love and power of God to redeem, cleanse, and set the captives free. Before a person becomes a Christian, their epic failures set the stage for an epic testimony of God's grace.

The poster child for this was the Apostle Paul. Before he came to Christ, he was Saul of Tarsus, "breathing threats and murder against the disciples of the Lord" (Acts 9:1). In 1 Timothy 1, he describes himself in those unsaved days as a "blasphemer and a persecutor and a violent aggressor" (1 Timothy 1:13). When it came to Christ and Christians, Saul was a bad dude. He was the worst of the worst as he tried to eradicate Christianity from the face of the earth.

No doubt, the early church was praying for God to thwart him and remove him. But God had other plans. He wasn't going to remove Saul, He was going to save Saul. He was going to change his life from top to bottom and make him a trophy of grace. You see, if the Lord can save the chief of sinners, Paul's designation of himself, He can save anyone!

A trophy of grace is a pretty cool way to be remembered, is it not?

There are many other such trophies of grace in the Bible and beyond. There are numerous stories of people who did violent, hateful, despicable things but came to Christ in repentance and faith and became new creations in Jesus. One such man was David Berkowitz, the so-called "Son of Sam" killer. During the summer of 1976, he terrorized the streets of New York City, killing six people and wounding seven others before being apprehended by the police. In prison, Berkowitz was befriended by a Christian and given a Gideon New Testament with Psalms and Proverbs. One night alone in his cell, Berkowitz was reading in the Psalms. As he read from Psalm 34:6, "This poor man cried, and the LORD heard him, and saved him out of all his troubles," Berkowitz broke down in tears before the Lord. He cried out for mercy and grace—and God, who is rich in mercy and grace, saved this undeserving murderer.

A trophy of God's grace? You bet. And we thank God for his salvation!

Karla Faye Tucker, the well-known murderess from Texas, also found Jesus Christ and forgiveness in prison. Before her arrest, she used a pickaxe to brutally murder two people sleeping in their beds. It was gruesome and awful. But the Lord gloriously saved her and transformed her life. She is a trophy of His grace.

We also might mention Jeffrey Dahmer, the man responsible for the deaths of seventeen people. Dahmer was found guilty of sexual assault, murder, necromancy, and cannibalism. He was eventually killed in prison, but before he went to meet his Maker, he professed his newfound faith in Jesus Christ. Could the Lord save a man as evil and wicked as Jeffrey Dahmer? Is there salvation for someone like him? Yes! The blood of Jesus can cleanse the worst of sinners who come in repentance and faith. While I do not pretend to know what is in a man's heart (Dahmer may or may not have been sincere), I do know that Jesus can save and will save anyone who comes to Him broken and repentant, as the prostitute in Luke 7 did. Hallelujah! What a Savior!

But what about a Christian who has an epic failure? How about a saved person who takes a tremendous fall, betrays a trust, breaks people's hearts, and lets others down? Is a person like that finished and written off as damaged goods? Is he or she disqualified from serving Christ ever again?

We don't have to look through newspaper clippings to find someone like that as an example. We only have to look in the pages of our New Testament. The Apostle Peter, the leader of the twelve apostles, experienced an epic moral failure, and we can learn much from his experience.

Not as Strong as He Thought

Our story begins on a Thursday night at an intimate, private meeting that has become known as the Last Supper. In Luke 22:31-34, we read this anguished conversation between the Lord and Peter, with Jesus speaking first:

> "Simon, Simon, behold, Satan has demanded permission to sift you like wheat; but I have prayed for you, that your faith may not fail; and you, when once you have turned again, strengthen your brothers." But he said to Him, "Lord, with You I am ready to go both to prison and to death!" And He said, "I say to you, Peter, the rooster will not crow today until you have denied three times that you know Me."

Fast-forwarding just a few hours, we read the outcome of that Upper Room conversation:

> Having arrested Him, they led Him away and brought Him to the house of the high priest, but Peter was following at a distance. After they had kindled a fire in the middle of the courtyard and sat down together, Peter was sitting among them. And a servant-girl, seeing him as he sat in the firelight and looking intently at him, said, "This man was with Him, too." But he

denied it, saying, "Woman, I do not know Him." A little later, another saw him and said, "You are one of them too!" But Peter said, "Man, I am not!" After about an hour had passed, another man began to insist, saying, "Certainly this man also was with Him, for he is a Galilean, too." But Peter said, "Man, I do not know what you are talking about." Immediately, while he was still speaking, a rooster crowed. The Lord turned and looked at Peter. And Peter remembered the word of the Lord, how He had told him, "Before a rooster crows today, you will deny Me three times." And he went out and wept bitterly.

—Luke 22:54-62

What do we learn from Simon Peter's epic failure? Four lessons that will serve as a great encouragement to every true believer.

Lesson 1: Epic Failures Can Easily Sneak Up on Us

In Matthew's account, Jesus looked at the men around the table and told them bluntly, "You will all fall away because of Me this night, for it is written." (Matthew 26:31)

I don't think we have any idea how stunning that statement must have been to the men in that room. Shocked almost beyond words, they all quickly denied it. Peter, however, really got riled up about it, pushing back with passionate indignation. He boldly declared, *"Even* though all may fall away because of You, I will **never** fall away." (Matthew 26:33)

Be careful with that word *never.*

Then he added these words: "Even if I have to die with You, I will not deny You!" (Matthew 26:35). Peter thought there was no way that could *possibly* happen to him. He couldn't imagine or conceive of such a failure, the failure of denying his Lord.

But it happened anyway, just as Jesus told him it would. So, what do we glean from this aspect of his failure?

We need to be careful of our boasts.

Peter has vehemently stated, "Lord, these other guys might turn tail and run, but I never will." Now, was he dissing the other disciples and throwing his Christian brothers under the bus? No, he was just trying to make a point that he felt very strongly at that moment. "Lord, You can count on me. You have no idea how committed I am to You!"

Peter was a take-charge guy. A true leader. In his mind, he was the Lord's go-to guy. He had confidence in himself and confidence in his commitment and resolve. But it really boiled down to this: Peter had confidence in the flesh. And when it was put to the test, his confidence melted "like a snow cone in Phoenix." (Kudos to Mrs. Doubtfire [Robin Williams] for teaching me that line.)

Be careful of your boasts. Be careful of saying what you would never, ever, not in a million years do. Don't even go there. Just make sure to walk in the strength, power, and awareness of the Holy Spirit every day of your life. In 1 Corinthians 10:12, Paul wrote: "Therefore let him who thinks he stands take heed that he does not fall." In the book of Proverbs, Solomon declared, "Pride goes before destruction, and a haughty spirit before stumbling."

When we think we have it in the bag, when we're telling the Lord and others, "No worries, I've got this whipped," that's when we're on thin ice. If you think you stand, if you think you're finally on solid ground, if you keep telling yourself you have put all your old sinful tendencies behind you, be careful! We all have feet of clay, and no one is immune to temptation and sin. In our flesh, we are capable of just about anything. Be cautious about making statements or claims that grow out of your own self-confidence.

Peter had said to the Lord, "Even if I have to die with You, I will never deny You" (Matthew 26:35, CSB).

Anytime you and I start following the Lord at a distance, we're in trouble. We desperately need to stay close to Him.

Pastor Jeff

But Jesus told him, "Truly I say to you, that this very night, before a rooster crows twice, you yourself will deny Me three times." (Mark 14:30)

We need to be careful of following at a distance.

Luke 22:54 says, "And having arrested Him (Jesus), they led Him away and brought Him to the house of the high priest; but Peter was following at a distance."

Anytime you and I start following the Lord at a distance, we're in trouble. We desperately need to stay close to Him. We need close proximity and heart-to-heart intimacy with Him. In the Psalms, Asaph writes, "But as for me, the **nearness** of God is my good." (Psalm 73:28)

If we come to a place in life where we are following from a distance, we will find ourselves getting further and further away from Jesus. Before long, He will be out of sight, over the horizon, and we will no longer sense His presence. Our daily quiet times will turn into weekly quiet times, and our prayer times become more and more hurried and distracted. Before we know it, we're just going through the motions and moving closer than we realize to serious trouble.

This well-worn statement is certainly true: If you follow Jesus from a distance, it won't be long before you're not following Him at all.

Do you remember what Jesus told the disciples when He went to the Garden of Gethsemane? "Remain here and keep watch with Me. The spirit is willing, but the flesh is weak" (Matthew 26:38,41). And what was Peter doing? He was sleeping—sleeping when he should have been praying.

The Lord told him, "Truly I say to you, that this very night, before a rooster crows twice, you yourself will deny Me three times" (Mark 14:30). The cock crowed twice at 3:00 a.m., so the Lord was saying, in effect, "Before 3:00 a.m., this is what's going to happen." If Peter really believed that, he would have certainly found a way to stay awake and plead with God for strength. But he didn't believe it—not really—and

> *He knows the end from the beginning (Isaiah 46:10). God sees your whole life, and He knows what you're going to do before you ever do it.*

he didn't take the time to pray against the powerful satanic attack coming his way.

Lesson 2: Epic Failures Don't Surprise the Lord, but They Do Hurt Him

Peter's great failure may have been a surprise to Peter, but it wasn't to Jesus. He had already told Peter what was coming, both at the Last Supper and then again on their way to Gethsemane. *Watch out, Peter! Satan has designs on you. You are about to walk into a trap.*

Remember this about the Lord: He knows the end from the beginning (Isaiah 46:10). God sees your whole life, and He knows what you're going to do before you ever do it. As David wrote, "You understand my thought from afar. Even before there is a word on my tongue, Behold, O LORD, You know it all." (Psalm 139:2, 4)

However, don't get the wrong idea here. Just because the Lord told Peter what he was going to do, that did not mean the Lord *made* him do it. Not at all. The Lord didn't make him deny Jesus, and He certainly did not want him to commit that great sin. He just knew in His foreknowledge what was about to happen.

Foreknowledge doesn't mean God has you trapped in some kind of pattern, and because you are "predestined" to do something, you have no choice. No, you *always* have a choice. But God already knows what you will choose because He knows the end from the beginning. He is the all-knowing, Sovereign God.

Even so, just because Jesus knew his close friend was about to betray Him, it didn't take away the pain and anguish He felt when it happened. When I had knee surgery many years ago, my orthopedic surgeon told me point blank that it would hurt—and it did. Knowing what was coming did not lessen the pain. And the same was true with Jesus.

Matthew's gospel tells us in Chapter 26 that after Jesus was arrested in the Garden of Gethsemane, He was dragged to the house of the high priest, where He was manhandled, beaten, spit on, and lied about. Scripture says He was led into the courtyard, and Peter, who had been following at a safe distance, finally ended up in the same courtyard.

Drawn by the warmth of a fire, Peter stepped forward with the intention of warming himself. He probably imagined himself coming in under the radar, staying quiet, and keeping an eye on the proceedings. *But why in the world was that servant girl staring at him in the firelight?* Finally, pointing her finger at Peter, she said, "This man was with Him, too!"

The girl's sudden accusation caught Peter off guard. He wasn't at all ready for a sudden, direct attack coming out of nowhere. He might have been imagining himself called before the Sanhedrin at some point. They would be saying, "Jesus, is there no one to give testimony for You?" And then maybe Jesus would call him up, and he would stand in front of everyone and declare, "You are the Christ, the Son of the living God," as he once did.

But he wasn't ready for a servant-girl in the courtyard saying, "You're one of them." It wasn't at all how he had visualized everything that would develop. For crying out loud, he was just standing by a fire, getting his hands warm!

Surprised as he was, he just shook his head and denied it all. "What? Who? No, I don't know Him. You don't know what you're talking about."

Flustered and frustrated, he went away from the fire and walked down a corridor that led closer to the gate to get away from those people. But then another servant-girl said, "You're one of them."

What was up with these servant girls?

"No, I don't know Him. No, no, you don't know what you're talking about. I don't even understand what you're saying." And then, about an hour later, another bystander approached him. In John's gospel, he tells us that it was a family member of Malchus.

Remember Malchus? A servant of the high priest, he was the guy who Peter tried to split in two with a sword back in the Garden of Gethsemane. Peter's aim was off, however, and he only succeeded in slicing off the man's right ear. Jesus had said to him, "Put the sword into the sheath; the cup which the Father has given Me, am I not to drink it?" (John 18:11). The gospel of Luke tells us that Jesus put the man's ear back in place and healed him on the spot. Wow!

So, this relative of Malchus confronted Peter, saying, "Did I not see you in the garden with Him?" (John 18:26). At this, the gospel of Matthew tells us, "Then he began to curse and swear, 'I do not know the man!'" (Matthew 26:74)

Cursing and swearing? Does this mean Peter let loose with a string of expletives? Could this seasoned fisherman of Galilee cuss like a sailor? Well, perhaps he could, but this is not what he did here. In fact, what he did at that moment was much worse. He said, in effect, "I swear by the living God that I do not know this Jesus. And if I am lying, may the curses of God come down upon me." Yikes!

Scripture says while those words were leaving his mouth, a rooster crowed. And then we come to Luke 22:61, which has to be one of the most devastating verses in the New Testament.

"And then the Lord turned and looked at Peter."

They locked eyes. Jesus saw Peter, and Peter saw Jesus. He saw the One whose face was bloodied and swollen from the beatings and wet with the spit of His accusers. And in that incredible moment, just as Jesus was being led through the courtyard to the house of the high priest, He turned and looked at him.

What do you suppose was in that look?

Surprise? No, there was no surprise because Jesus already knew what Peter was going to do. Was it a look of, "I told you so?" No, there was no need for that. I believe it was a look of wounded love. Without ever saying a word, His look conveyed, *"Peter, when I needed you the most, you denied that you even knew Me."*

Until his dying day, I don't imagine Peter ever forgot that moment. All he could do was stumble outside and cry his eyes out. The mere look of Jesus Christ, the one he truly loved yet denied, had shattered his heart.

Adrian Rogers once said that the difference between a true and false believer is this: "A slave fears the lash, but a son fears the father's displeasure." In a brief encounter that may have only lasted a few seconds at most, Peter experienced the tremendous hurt in the Lord's eyes, and it cut him to the quick.

Lesson 3: Epic Failures Usher in the Lies of the Devil

It was Satan, of course, who had orchestrated all this pain and devastation. It was the devil's big night, and he must have been savoring every moment of it. At last! Revenge on God's Son and all who followed Him. As Jesus had specifically told Peter: "Simon, Simon, behold, Satan has demanded permission to sift you like wheat" (Luke 22:31).

"Simon, Simon." This is the only place in Scripture where Jesus said Simon Peter's name twice. Typically, when your name gets repeated, it isn't good. In Luke 10, Jesus also repeated Martha's name as He gently rebuked her for worrying and having misplaced priorities. "Simon, Simon," Jesus said, and then He gave him the ominous news. The Lord was going to allow the devil to come after him hard. Satan was going to violently shake Simon Peter, like the violent shaking that occurs when one separates the wheat from the chaff.

> *The blood of Jesus, God's Son, cleanses from*
>
> *all sin, no matter how terrible.*

In later years, Peter himself would write the warning: "Be of sober spirit, be on the alert. Your adversary, the devil, prowls around like a roaring lion, seeking someone to devour" (1 Peter 5:8). On the night of the Lord's arrest, the devil roared at Peter, and Peter feared greatly and fell like a ton of bricks.

Then came the crushing tsunami of regret, along with all of the recriminations and self-loathing. The devil moved in to accuse and accuse, just as he always does. At that moment, the adversary was trying to cut Peter's legs out from under him. He was doing his best to take out the number one disciple. What was Satan's ultimate goal? I think it was more than just getting Peter to deny Jesus; I think he wanted Peter to follow in the footsteps of Judas, who betrayed the Lord, was filled with remorse, *and then went out and hanged himself.* The devil was aiming at Peter's total destruction. He wanted to smash this follow-Christ movement before it ever got started.

What kind of fake news was he broadcasting at that moment? You've probably heard it many times yourself.

First, he said, *"You can never be truly forgiven.* Just look at what you did! Look at how you failed. What you did was unforgivable! Denying Jesus just when He needed you most? And then doing it *three times?* And after all your boasts? That's beyond the pale. Let's stick a fork in you. You are done, pal."

It's a lie, of course. Peter could be forgiven and was forgiven. And so can you. The blood of Jesus, God's Son, cleanses from *all* sin, no matter how terrible—even the terrible sin of denying Christ in His hour of need.

The Lord says in Isaiah 1:18:

> "'Come now, and let us reason together,' Says the LORD,
> 'Though your sins are as scarlet, They will be as white as snow;
> Though they are red like crimson, They will be like wool.'"

As the age-old hymn "To God Be the Glory" so eloquently expresses, "The vilest offender who truly believes, that moment from Jesus a pardon receives." It's the same for a Christian who has fallen into epic failure. The same Lord washes all sin, even the worst of sin, whiter than snow.[1]

Another tactic the enemy likes to use when we commit the worst of transgressions goes something like this: "Well, you might be forgiven. But it doesn't change what you've done. The Lord will forgive you, but it will never be the same. You will never have the relationship you once had. He might let you in the back door, but you will be a second-class Christian for the rest of your life. There will be an asterisk by your name in the Lamb's book of life."

In an earlier chapter, I mentioned the story of the prodigal son found in Luke 15. Perhaps you remember the story of how he greatly dishonored his father by saying something to this effect: "Dad, I can't just sit around any longer, waiting for you to die. I'm burning daylight here. How about you give me my inheritance now?" And so, he took his father's money and went out and wasted it on wine, women, and song.

He ended up losing everything. And when a severe famine hit the land, the only work he could secure was feeding a local farmer's pigs. Already near starvation, he started thinking the pig slop he was pouring into the swine troughs was looking pretty good.

And then he came to his senses. He said to himself, "Wait a minute! My father's hired men on the farm get three square meals a day. What am I doing here, dying of hunger?" After thinking about it for a minute or two, he said, "This is what I'm going to do. I'm going home. I'm going to go see my dad, and I'm going to say to him, 'Dad, I have sinned against heaven

---

[1] Footnote: Fanny J. Crosby. "To God Be The Glory." 1875.

and in your sight. I'm not worthy to be called your son, let me work for you like one of your hired men" (Luke 15:18-19). Obviously, working for his dad would be much better than working at the pig sty. In one of the most poignant moments in the New Testament, Jesus said that the father saw his boy when he was a long way off. And undignified as it was, the old man hiked up his robe, embarrassingly exposing his legs, and started running. He ran to his son, embraced him, and kissed him. As the son began his well-rehearsed speech, his dad stopped him mid-sentence. What a sweet interruption that was! Scripture records it like this:

> "But the father said to his slaves, 'Quickly bring out the best robe and put it on him, and put a ring on his finger and sandals on his feet; and bring the fattened calf, slaughter it, and let's eat and celebrate; for this son of mine was dead and has come to life again; he was lost and has been found.'"

> —Luke 15:22-23

Maybe you have been listening to the devil's fake news and hearing him say, "God might forgive you partially, but it will never be the same between you again. You will be like hired help in His house, but that's all. He will want you to keep your distance."

Years ago, a friend of mine experienced a marriage breakup. We spent some fun time together in those days playing racquetball and shooting the breeze (casually conversing). I could tell that the Lord was working on his heart.

"Jeff," he told me, "every morning of my life I get up and ask God to forgive me for the way I treated my ex-wife. Every day, I say, 'Oh, God, would you forgive me for those terrible things I said and did to her?" And then he would begin to tell me how awful he had been.

One time, I said to him, "You do that every morning?"

"Yeah, I do."

I said, "How about doing this? Instead of confessing those same sins a thousand times, why don't you start thanking God a thousand times for forgiving you of those sins?"

As mere humans, it is all too easy to continue to feel guilt, shame, and condemnation even after we have asked God for forgiveness. To be sure, we don't instantly feel forgiven because we still must deal with the consequences of our sinful choices. And when we don't *feel* forgiven, we believe the enemies' lies that we aren't forgiven, and we rightly deserve the continual guilt and shame that we are experiencing.

But here is the real truth: when we have come before the Lord in genuine humility and repentance, and have asked Him to forgive us— He does! First John 1:9 tells us, "If we confess our sins, He is faithful and righteous to forgive us our sins and cleanse us from all unrighteouesness." God's forgiveness is not partial, it is complete and total. Every part of our sin is cleansed and washed away, if and when we truly confess it to Him.

So, we must make an intentional choice not to continue walking in shame but to start walking in the amazing forgiveness He has granted us.

The devil will tell you, "You can never be used again. You'd better get used to riding the bench for the rest of your life."

But that's a lie, too! Proverbs 24:16 tells us that "a righteous man falls seven times, and rises again." We're talking here about a *righteous* person—not a bum or a scum or an unbeliever loser—someone made right with God by faith in the Lord. Even righteous people fall, even seven times! And when we fall and fail over and over, we rise again! We don't stay down!

I once heard the late Jerry Falwell say, "It's always too early to quit." But that's exactly what Satan wants you to do. After an epic failure, he wants you to say, "I can't do it. I can't show my face again. I can't go to church again. I'm better off dead." He told that to Peter, too, but fifty days later, Peter courageously stood up on the Day of Pentecost, preached a powerful message, and thousands were saved.

The Lord wasn't done with Peter, and He's not done with you.

Lesson 4: Epic Failures Require Genuine Repentance and True Faith

Scripture says that after Peter's failure, he "remembered the word of the Lord, how He had told him, 'Before a rooster crows today, you will deny Me three times.' And he went out and wept bitterly." (Luke 22:61)

There was tremendous pain in his heart for what he did, and Peter grieved over it. But he also got right with God again. And how did he do that? Through repentance and faith.

If you have had an epic failure in your life, you can get right with God. A lost person can come to Jesus and get right with Him, and so can a saved person. How does it happen?

Scripture tells us we must have *godly sorrow*, not just *worldly regret*. There's a big difference. In 2 Corinthians 7:10 we read: "For the sorrow that is according to *the will of* God produces a repentance without regret, *leading* to salvation, but the sorrow of the world produces death." You might underline that verse in your Bible and write "Peter vs. Judas" over the top of it.

Peter had godly sorrow that produced repentance. Judas had worldly regret that produced death. Judas was sorry for what he did and regretted what he did, but he didn't repent. He didn't have true faith. Jesus said, "Did I not choose you, the twelve, and yet one of you is a devil?" (John 6:70). That one was Judas.

Judas was overwhelmed with remorse. As Adrian Rogers poignantly stated, "Trying to escape the hell within him . . . Judas hung himself and stepped into the hell before him." Peter didn't go that route. Peter had godly sorrow. Was he deeply wounded inside over what he had done? You'd better believe it! By crying out for God's mercy and turning from his sin, he found true forgiveness and restoration in the Lord.[2]

But then, not only did he have godly sorrow and genuine repentance,

---

[2] Footnote: Adrian Rogers. "Why Did Jesus Choose Judas Iscariot to Be a Disciple?" Love Worth Finding Ministries. Accessed 16 October 204. URL.

but he also had true faith. Jesus had given him a word of hope, and he clung to that with all his might. Remember the Lord's words in the Upper Room? "Simon, Simon, behold, Satan has demanded permission to sift you like wheat; *but I have prayed for you, that your faith may not fail;* and you, *when once you have turned again*, strengthen your brothers." (Luke 22:31-32, emphasis mine)

That was a word from the Lord before he ever failed, and I imagine he went back to that statement a thousand times. *The Lord has prayed for me. The Lord prayed that my faith wouldn't fail. The Lord told me that I would turn again, and strengthen my brothers. Praise God, there is hope for me!*

His faith couldn't fail because it was founded on the Rock, the Lord Jesus Christ. None of us has been saved by our works; we are saved by our faith anchored in Christ. And Peter himself tells us that we are "protected by the power of God through faith." (1 Peter 1:5)

Why did the Lord allow the devil to step in and try to destroy Simon Peter? It was to show him that true faith never fails.

You might say Peter had a total *eclipse* of his faith, much like an eclipse of the sun where everything grows dark as night. After his shameful denials, he probably couldn't even see his faith for a while. But it was an eclipse of faith, not a collapse.

After an eclipse, the sun returns, as bright as ever. It is darkness, yes, but a temporary darkness. Why? Because Peter was a true believer in Jesus and he remembered and believed in the Lord's words to him. He *would* turn again, and he *would* strengthen his brothers.

One of my favorite parts of the resurrection story, detailed in all four gospels, is the account found in Mark. The early church fathers made it known that Mark wrote Peter's gospel. While the Gospel of Mark is truly inspired by the Holy Spirit, his writing came from the details Peter provided him. It was at the empty tomb, where the women encountered the angel and heard these words: "Do not be amazed; you are looking for Jesus the Nazarene, who has been crucified. He has risen; He is not here; behold,

God can still use you. You are not a hired hand or a second-class citizen. No! You are a beloved son, a beloved daughter.

here is the place where they laid Him. But go, tell His disciples and Peter, 'He is going ahead of you to Galilee; there you will see Him, behold, I have told you.'" (Mark 16:6-7)

"Go tell His disciples AND PETER. . . . "

Can't you just imagine how those exhilarating words set off fireworks in Peter's heart? "I'm still included! He hasn't given up on me! He still has a plan for me!"

Go tell His disciples . . . *and Peter!*

Or maybe, go tell His disciples . . . *and Jeff.*

You can insert your own name in that sentence. He wasn't done with Peter, and He's not done with you. Cling to the hope of His Word and keep trusting and following Him. My friend and former president of Family Life Ministries, Dennis Rainey, once wrote, "So what have you done that disqualifies you from being used by God? Answer: If you have repented, nothing!"

God can still use you. You are not a hired hand or a second-class citizen. No! You are a beloved son, a beloved daughter. The Father is thrilled with your coming to Him, repenting, and turning from your sin. He will wash you, cleanse you, restore you, and use you once again to advance His kingdom in these final days before He returns.

It's time for us to reject and silence our adversary's fake news, to stand up for the truth, to believe the truth, and to walk in that truth.

No matter what you've done, you're not disqualified from serving Jesus. God still has a plan for you.

Let me close this chapter with a poem I ran across a number of years ago. It is from the French cleric, Michael Quoist (1918 – 1997). It so aptly addresses the guilt and shame we feel when we fall and fail in some huge way. May the words he writes minister to your heart.

I have fallen, Lord,
Once more.
I can't go on, I'll never succeed.
I am ashamed, I don't dare look at you.
And yet I struggled, Lord, for I knew you were right near me,
bending over me, watching.
But temptation blew like a hurricane,
And instead of looking at you I turned my head away,
I stepped aside
While you stood, silent and sorrowful,
Like the spurned lover who sees his loved one carried away to the
enemy.
When the wind died down as suddenly as it had arisen,
When the lightning ceased after proudly streaking the darkness,
All of a sudden I found myself alone, ashamed, disgusted, with
my sin in my hands.
This sin that I selected the way a customer makes his purchase,
This sin that I have paid for and cannot return, for the shopkeep-
er is no longer there,
This tasteless sin,
This odorless sin,
This sin that sickens me,
That I have wanted but want no more,
That I have imagined, sought, played with, fondled, for a long time;
That I have finally embraced while turning coldly away from you,
My arms outstretched, my eyes and heart irresistibly drawn;
This sin that I have grasped and consumed with gluttony,

It's mine now, but it possesses me as the spiderweb holds captive
the gnat.
It is mine,
It sticks to me,
It flows in my veins,
It fills my heart.
It has slipped in everywhere, as darkness slips into the forest at dusk
And fills all the patches of light.
I can't get rid of it.
I run from it the way one tries to lose a stray dog, but it catches
up with me and bounds joyfully against my legs.
Everyone must notice it.
I'm so ashamed that I feel like crawling to avoid being seen,
I'm ashamed of being seen by my friends,
I'm ashamed of being seen by you, Lord,
For you loved me, and I forgot you.
I forgot you because I was thinking of myself
And one can't think of several persons at once.
One must choose, and I chose.
And your voice,
And your look
And your love hurt me.
They weigh me down
They weigh me down more than my sin.
Lord, don't look at me like that,
For I am naked,
I am dirty,
I am down,
Shattered,
With no strength left.
I dare make no more promises,

I can only lie bowed before you.

God responds . . .

Come, son, my child, look up!
Isn't it mainly your pride that is wounded?
If you loved me, you would grieve, but you would trust.
Do you think that there's a limit to God's love?
Do you think that for a moment I stopped loving you?
But you still rely on yourself, son. You must rely only on me.
Ask my pardon
And get up quickly.
You see, it's not falling that is the worst,
But staying on the ground.[3]

---

[3]Footnote: Michel Quoist. "I Have Fallen." *Grace Space*. Accessed November 19, 2024. https://www.justprayer.gracespace.info/i-have-fallen-michel-quoist/.

-8-

The Real *Inconvenient Truth*

*"I was dead, and behold, I am alive forevermore,
and I have the keys of death and of Hades."*
—REVELATION 1:18

In 2006, Al Gore, former Vice President, presidential candidate, self-proclaimed inventor of the Internet, and now full-time environmentalist, released a movie called *An Inconvenient Truth.*

You may remember that the movie was concerned with global warming. Gore portrayed our planet in an advanced state of crisis, insisting that if we don't do something soon to reduce our carbon dioxide emissions, earth will become too warm, the ice caps will melt, the polar bears will perish, and everything will pretty much disintegrate. The movie had a budget of $1.5 million and took in almost $50 million at the box office.

That film may have worked very well for Al Gore's bottom line, but what does the Bible say about this idea of man causing the end of the world? It's pretty clear. *God* is in control of this earth and what happens to it, *not* man. In Genesis 8:22, the Lord declares (with complete authority):

"While the earth remains,
Seedtime and harvest,

> *God is in control of this earth and*
>
> *what happens to it, not man.*

And cold and heat,
And summer and winter,
And day and night
Shall not cease."

Man won't bring an end to human existence by driving an SUV or using plastic straws. Conversely, man won't prolong the planet by using more solar panels or having everyone become a vegetarian. I think of this 'inconvenient truth' as a convenient fabrication because Al Gore got very rich off the movie's box office. His net worth today rings in at around $300 million dollars.

I could list many other 'inconvenient truths' in our world today, but there is one very inconvenient truth that everyone must deal with. It is the *real* inconvenient truth that Satan doesn't want you to hear, believe, or even think about.

It is the reality of a place called hell.

Not long ago, the pastor of one of America's largest congregations was asked point-blank, "Do you ever preach on hell?"

"No," he said, "I don't."

"Why not?"

"Because I don't want to make people feel bad. I want to make people feel good. People already know that they're doing bad, so why do I want to come and talk to them about hell?" And so, he never talks about it. He never warns people of the reality of hell.

Ironically, the preacher who spoke the most about hell was the one who loved people the most, laying down His life for all of us: Jesus Christ. Jesus spoke about hell often in His teachings. In fact, the argument can be made that Jesus talked more about hell than He did about heaven (it depends on how you count the verses). Honest scholars can disagree here, but they can't disagree on the undeniable truth that Jesus believed in a place called hell. He sternly warned of hell because He doesn't want anyone to go there. Hell is an unspeakably awful place; words cannot begin to adequately describe its horrors. The topic of hell and divine retribution is an often omitted but sorely needed subject for our world today. As someone once said, "If the pulpits in America spent more time talking about hell, the streets in America wouldn't see so much hell practiced out in public."

In my studies, I once ran across an anonymous and insightful quote concerning the moral degradation in Great Britain following World War II: "The moral landslide in Great Britain can be traced back to the fact that heaven and hell are no longer proclaimed in the land." In *Newsweek* magazine, August 12, 2002, Kenneth Woodward wrote about the absence of hell in pulpits across America. He titled his article, "Why We Need Hell, Too: Churchgoers Take Comfort: Hell Has All But Disappeared From Modern Christian Theology."[1] How shocking that even secular writers understood the importance of warning people about hell.

In Luke 12:4, Jesus spoke these sobering words: "I say to you, My friends, do not be afraid of those who kill the body and after that have no more that they can do. But I will warn you whom to fear: fear the One who, after He has killed, has authority to cast into hell; yes, I tell you, fear Him!"

On its face, this is a frightening statement. But we live in a world today where people don't fear God and don't fear hell. Since they rarely if ever hear about hell from their pastors and teachers, they're not very concerned about it. Out of sight, out of mind. Although a 2023 Gallup poll revealed that 59% of Americans still believe in hell, down from 71% in 2003, very few people think they are going there. George Barna's 2003 research showed that only

---

[1] Footnote: Kenneth L. Woodward "Why We Need Hell, Too: Churchgoers Take Comfort: Hell Has All but Disappeared from Modern Christian Theology." *Newsweek*, August 12, 2002.

Although, 59% of Americans still believe in hell, very few people think they are going there. Research showed that only 0.5% of Americans believed that they would end up in hell, and 64% were relatively confident that they would go to heaven.

0.5% of Americans believed that they would end up in hell. Conversely, 64% were relatively confident that they would go to heaven.

In 2010, a book came out titled *Heaven Is for Real: A Little Boy's Astounding Story of His Trip to Heaven and Back.* It quickly became a bestseller with over ten million in book sales within a couple of years. In 2014, the book was turned into a movie. People love to hear stories that heaven is for real. But what would happen if someone wrote a book called *Hell Is for Real* to detail their experiences in hell? Would that stir up the same enthusiastic fervor? Would Hollywood be clamoring to turn that depressing story into a full length feature film? Probably not. People don't want to think about or talk about hell. It is not a pleasant consideration.

But the truth of the matter is unavoidable, whether you want to think about it or not. And, if you believe the Bible, there is really no way to get around it. Hell is for real, just as heaven is for real. These are fixed realities proclaimed by the Lord Jesus Christ, who is the very embodiment of truth.

We're wrapping up this book called *The Devil's Newsroom* where we have been considering the deceptions and devices of an ancient and powerful spirit being whom the Bible calls "the devil, and Satan" (Revelation 12:9). Jesus called him a murderer and "the father of lies" (John 8:44). In this final chapter, we've come to one of his most evil, cruel, and destructive lies of all. We could call this his ultimate deception. And what is his ultimate deception?

There is no hell.

This lie takes many forms. People will say things like, "There is no life after death." Or maybe, "God is a God of love, and everyone makes it to heaven eventually."

But if we say things like that, we're no longer saying what the Bible says. We're no longer agreeing with Jesus. We're out on our own, betting our eternal destiny on a false reality of our own making.

The Bible truly does teach about a place called hell. What does it say about it, exactly? Let's look at three important discoveries.

Discovery #1: Hell is a Real Place

The place called hell is not a figment of someone's imagination or a concoction of some fired-up evangelist trying to scare people into making a decision for Christ. Hell is a real place that really exists.

What is it like in hell? Here are four particulars straight from the New Testament.

Hell is a place of eternal fire.

That's how Jesus described it. In Mark 9:43, He says this:

> "If your hand causes you to stumble, cut it off; it is better for you to enter life crippled, than, having your two hands, to go into hell, into the unquenchable fire."

It's called unquenchable fire, eternal fire, the furnace of fire, and the lake of fire. Without question, hell is described as fire. In the gospel of Luke, Jesus gave an account of a rich man who died and went to a place the New American Standard Bible calls Hades. The King James calls it hell. Is there a difference? Yes. Hades isn't the eternal abode of unbelievers, hell is. Although both places are very similar, one is temporary, and one is not. Think of it this way: if you commit a terrible, capital crime, you are arrested and taken to the county jail to await your hearing before the judge. Upon hearing your case, the judge concludes you are guilty, and sentences you to life in prison. Hades is the holding place of the unrighteous dead. It is the county jail. Hell is the state penitentiary. It is the place that houses you for all eternity. Regardless of the technicality, neither place is fun and games. We could rightly say that both places are "hot as hell." In Luke 16:24, the rich man (*Dives* in Latin) who went to Hades confessed, "I am in agony in this flame!"

The Greek word for "hell" used eleven times in the gospels of Matthew, Mark, and Luke is *gehenna*. Gehenna was a place known in the Old Testament as the Valley of Hinnom, or Gehinnom. It was the name given to a narrow valley or glen southwest of Jerusalem where some of the ungodly, idolatrous kings of Judah would sacrifice their own sons and daughters as a burnt offering to the false god, Molech. It was a ghastly, abhorrent practice in Israel that persisted until God raised up a righteous reformer king named Josiah, who did away with it.

When the Valley of Hinnom ceased being a place of pagan sacrifices, it became a city dump where people would burn their refuse. Smoke would always rise from that national dumpster fire because it smoldered and burned continually. When Jesus spoke of hell using the word 'gehenna,' people understood exactly what He meant: an evil place where the fire never goes out.

Sometimes, you hear people mock the idea of hell. You will hear someone say, "Well, hell doesn't sound so bad to me. All my friends will be there. We'll sit around, drink beer, and play poker." Really? How many people do you know sit around and play poker in a blast furnace? Hell is a place of eternal fire.

Hell is a place of outer darkness.

Three times in the gospels, Jesus describes hell as a place of outer darkness.

Do you remember the ninth plague that came upon the Egyptians recorded in the book of Exodus? The Lord said to Moses in Exodus 10:21: "Stretch out your hand toward the sky, that there may be darkness over the land of Egypt, even a darkness *which may be felt.*"

Have you ever been deep in a cave or cavern somewhere—a place where no surface light can penetrate? If so, then you have a pretty good idea of what "a darkness which may be felt" is like. When I went on a mission trip to the Philippines a few years ago, we ministered in Palawan, a beautiful area with wonderful people! The church we were working with took us on a one-day excursion to the underground river in Puerto Princessa. We got on a canoe and traveled to a large cave that is home to millions of bats—I am not a fan of bats! This was truly "the bat cave." When we were quite a distance inside, I asked the man running the boat if he could turn out the big light mounted on the stern. He really didn't want to do it, but I said, "Please, I just want to see what this is like."

After just a few seconds, I was ready to have him turn the light back on again. A deep, overwhelming darkness fell over our canoe. You've heard people say, "It was so dark I couldn't see my hand in front of my face." But this time, it really was true. For a brief few seconds, I experienced a frightening darkness that could be felt.

That's how the Lord describes hell. It's a place of eternal fire, but it's also a place of outer darkness.

Hell is a place of awful sounds.

Once again describing the horrors of hell, Jesus said it was a place of "weeping and gnashing of teeth." He used that phrase seven times in the gospels and six times in Matthew alone. We know what weeping is. But this isn't just sniffling, this is *wailing.* The weeping that takes place in hell is sobbing from the depths of a person's being. It's a great lament with loud cries. Weeping because opportunity has been lost and wailing because the day of salvation is over. It's too late. Your eternity is set.

And then, gnashing of teeth. What does that really mean? The term used for "gnash" comes from a root Greek word, *brocko,* which means "to grate the teeth in pain or rage." The people who end up in hell are screaming in pain and rage. In Acts chapter 7, the men in the Jewish ruling council, called the Sanhedrin, were so angry and enraged at the young man Stephen that they "gnashed their teeth at him"—just before hauling him out into the street to stone him to death.

People in hell are in pain, but they are also furious with God for doing this to them. Revelation 16 talks about the seven bowls of wrath that God's holy angels pour out upon the world of unbelievers—those who have rejected God and salvation in His Son. Listen to this description of the fourth bowl:

> "The fourth angel poured out his bowl upon the sun, and it was given to it to scorch men with fire. Men were scorched with fierce heat; and they blasphemed the name of God who has the power over these plagues, and they did not repent so as to give Him glory."
>
> —Revelation 16:8-9

They're gnawing their tongues in pain, they're blaspheming God, and the Bible says, "they did not repent so as to give Him glory"—even during that terrible judgment.

When I was a kid, growing up with older brothers, they would sometimes pin me down, pull my arm behind my back and yell, "Say Uncle! Say Uncle! When are you gonna say UNCLE?" I didn't *want* to say Uncle. I didn't *want* to give my brothers that satisfaction. But finally, it hurt so much that I would yell, "Okay! Okay! I tap out. I give up. I'm saying it. UNCLE!"

In Revelation 16, however, those in rebellion against God refuse to give in and can't bear to give God glory. So, they gnash their teeth in pain and in anger, growling out their blasphemies. I once heard someone say, "If you could pry off the sewer grate of hell and hear the sounds coming up from that place, you would run down the church aisle to get saved." Hell is a place of awful sounds.

Hell is a place of eternal death.

Revelation 20:14 speaks of hell as "the lake of fire" and "the second death."

Sheer oblivion and annihilation, of course, would be a welcome alternative in comparison to eternal punishment. Some people think, *Well, you know, when you die, that's it! You cease to exist. It's a big blank forever.*

In the 1971 hit "Imagine," John Lennon sang, "Imagine there's no heaven, it's easy if you try, no hell below us, above us only sky."

People might find some kind of perverse comfort in believing there is "no hell below us." But if you hold to the words of Jesus Christ, that option isn't open to you. Just as heaven is a place of eternal life, hell is a place of eternal death. Physical death is the separation of the spirit from the body. Spiritual death is the separation of the spirit from God.

Being separated forever from God is hell.

In 2 Thessalonians 1:7-9, the apostle Paul speaks of that day "when the Lord Jesus will be revealed from heaven with His mighty angels in flaming fire, dealing out retribution to those who do not know God and to those who do not obey the gospel of our Lord Jesus. These will pay the penalty of eternal destruction, away from the presence of the Lord and from the glory of His power."

Those are terrible, almost unthinkable words! And because hell is a place of eternal death, it's also a place of everlasting despair. Despair is an interesting word. It means 'the complete loss or absence of hope; desperation, anguish, and gloom.' No one ever has a good day in hell. No one

> *Physical death is the separation of the spirit from the body. Spiritual death is the separation of the spirit from God.*

ever looks forward to anything in hell. Every day is worse than the day before. In Dante Alighieri's ancient poem, The Divine Comedy, there is a sign above the portals of hell which reads, "Abandon hope, all ye who enter here."[2] How accurate and horrible.

No wonder people don't like to talk about the subject of hell. To be honest, I don't much like writing about it. It breaks my heart to think of this place. But it is very real. The Lord spoke of it with clarity.

So, the question arises in our minds . . . who are the people who go to hell?

Discovery #2: Hell is a populated place

Remember this about hell: God says that He created it "for the devil and his angels" (Matthew 25:41). God did not create hell for people, and He doesn't want people to go there. Tragically, they do go, however. You see, if someone continues walking in the footsteps of the devil and his fallen angels, that someone will end up where they end up—hell. According to Jesus, there are *many* who walk that disastrous road. In Matthew 7, He tells us: "Enter through the narrow gate; for the gate is wide and the way is broad that leads to destruction, and there are many who enter through it. For the gate is small and the way is narrow that leads to life, and there are few who find it." (Matthew 7:13-14)

---

[2]Footnote: Dante Alighieri. *The Divine Comedy*. 1320.

So, here is the tragedy: Most people are on that wrong road, the broad road that leads to destruction and hell. And almost all of these broad road travelers are clueless. Remember, the Barna research showed 0.5% of Americans think they are going to hell. That is why preachers and pastors who fail to talk about this *inconvenient truth* are doing their listeners such a grave disservice.

So, hell is a populated place. But who are the people who populate it? Who will be there?

Bad people will be there.

The Bible tells us that abominable people—murderers, liars, idolaters, and sorcerers—will be there (Revelation 21:8). That makes sense to us. We reason to ourselves, *Well, that's justice. That's where bad people need to go. Look at Adolf Hitler. Should he go to heaven for killing six million Jews? No! He deserves the fires of hell.* That's how our minds think. And, unless Hitler repented and turned to Jesus for salvation in his last moments, he will surely be in hell. Hell is filled with the Hitlers and the Herods, the Jezebels and the Judases, the Neros and the Nimrods. These are the notorious rebels against God who committed unspeakable atrocities against humanity. When Scripture uses the term "abominable," the word literally means "to stink." It's the foul, detestable, vile person, who stinks to high heaven. These individuals will be there in hell.

But here is the issue: Not only will hell be filled with bad people, but it will also be filled with "good" people. Why is the word good in quotes? Because there are no "good" people. The rich young ruler asked Jesus one day, "Good teacher, what shall I do to inherit eternal life?" But Jesus said to him, "Why do you call Me good? No one is good except God alone." (Luke 18:18-19). Romans 3:10 reaffirms this verse: "There is none righteous, not even one."

So, how many *good* people are there? Zero! "Well," someone might reply, "most people are good in comparison to Hitler or Osama Bin Laden."

We won't stand before God being compared to Hitler or some vicious terrorist. We will stand before God being compared to Jesus, the Holy One of Israel—and that makes for a whole different ballgame.

Pastor Jeff

In a sense, yes. But that's not the comparison that counts. We won't stand before God being compared to Hitler or some vicious terrorist. We will stand before God being compared to *Jesus*, the Holy One of Israel—and that makes for a whole different ballgame.

"Wait a minute! All of a sudden, I'm compared to Jesus? Jesus is without sin. Jesus is perfect. I'm not perfect!" Bingo, that's right. You're not good because no one is good except God alone. And Jesus is God. You're a sinner, I'm a sinner, and hell will be filled with "good people" who were depending on their "goodness" for salvation.

In every church, you have self-righteous people, people who trust in themselves and—even though they might never say it—think they are "good enough" by themselves to get to heaven. They acknowledge Jesus, but they don't trust in Jesus. They trust in themselves . . . in their good works . . . in their baptism . . . in their giving to the church . . . in their church activities . . . in the kind, sacrificial things they do for others. They trust in themselves.

Most of us have an aunt, an uncle, or a nice neighbor down the street whom we could describe as "just a sweet, good person." They're good neighbors with a cute little dog or cat, and they check on your house for you when you're on vacation. And we say to ourselves, "Surely, there's no way they could end up in hell because they're such *good people.*"

I like what Adrian Rogers once said on this subject: "The worst form of badness is human goodness, when that human goodness becomes a substitute for the new birth experience."[3]

Jesus said to Nicodemus, the most moral man of his day, "Truly, truly, I say to you, unless one is born again he cannot see the kingdom of God" (John 3:3). In other words, *I don't care how good you are, Nicodemus, or how many commandments you have kept. You have to be perfect to get into heaven because heaven is a perfect place, and no sin is allowed inside its gates.*

---

[3]Footnote: Adrian Rogers. "The Worst Form of Badness." Love Worth Finding Ministries, 4 December 2016. Accessed 16 October 2024. https://www.lwf.org/daily-devotions/the-worst-form-of-badness.

And that leaves every "good" person out. You can't get in with your goodness. You must be born again!

That was incredibly good news for Nicodemus that night, even if he didn't quite grasp it at the time.

And it's good news for you and me, too, as we look at the final discovery concerning hell.

Discovery #3: Hell is an avoidable place

No one has to go to hell. The Lord doesn't want people to go to hell. He says so very clearly in John 3:16: "For God so loved the world, that He gave His only begotten Son, that whoever believes in Him shall not perish, but have eternal life."

People have called that verse "the gospel in a nutshell," and it has to be in the running for the most familiar verse in the Bible. Even people who don't know much of the Bible tend to be somewhat familiar with John 3:16.

They may not know exactly what it says, but chances are they've seen or heard it somewhere. Former college and NFL star Tim Tebow used to write John 3:16 on his eye black on game day. Sometimes, people hold up "John 3:16" signs in the end zones.

What does that verse tell us?

It says that, apart from Christ, we are all perishing. We're pointed toward the worst of all disasters. Maybe you've heard someone say, "I don't believe that a loving God would ever create a hell, let alone send someone there." Or maybe, "If the Supreme Court of the United States could vote on this issue, they would outlaw hell as cruel and unusual punishment."

But they can't vote on it.

It's not up for a vote.

It doesn't matter what the United States government or the United Nations or CNN or the National Council of Churches has to say about it.

This place called hell is a reality. It exists.

Then why doesn't God do something about it?

He did. He gave His best. He gave His Son. He paid the price for each and every one of us so that we can escape hell and one day live with Him forever. God says in effect, "I'm going to put a cross right in the middle of that broad road that leads to destruction, and if any man, woman, boy, or girl ends up going to hell, they'll have to trip over the cross of Jesus Christ to get there."

Here's the good news—the best and most incomparably wonderful news: *If you come to Jesus for salvation, you will never, never, never go to hell.*

During Jesus's earthly ministry, He would look out at the crowd and say, "Come to Me, all who are weary and heavy-laden, and I will give you rest. Take My yoke upon you and learn from Me, for I am gentle and humble in heart, and you will find rest for your souls. For My yoke is easy and My burden is light." (Matthew 11:28-30)

Come to Me! What a beautiful, wide-open invitation. And then, in the last book of the Bible, at the end of time, we read:

> "The Spirit and the bride say, "Come." And let the one who hears say, "Come." And let the one who is thirsty come; let the one who wishes take the water of life without cost."

> —Revelation 22:17

Come! Come! COME!

You can come to Him. And if you come to Jesus, you will never go to hell.

When I was a very young Christian, someone gave me a book by Freddie Gage called *Pulpit in the Shadows.* Rev. Gage was a great evangelist for decades in the Southern Baptist Convention. In his early days, however, he was about as far away from the Lord as a young man could get.[4] Growing up on the mean streets of Houston, he became a gang leader

---

[4] Footnote: Freddie Gage. Pulpit in the Shadows. (Grand Rapids: Zondervan Publishing House, 1966)

and a first-class thug. His fellow hoodlums called him "The Cat." He was a violent criminal and proud of it, involving himself in drugs, burglary, vicious assaults, and prostitution.

One day, Freddie's dad surprised him. The older man said that Jesus Christ had completely changed his life, and he wanted Freddie to come to church with him. The younger Gage laughed in his dad's face. "I'm not going to church," he said. "That's for a bunch of hypocrites." But his dad persisted in praying for him and talking to him about Christ.

One day, his dad said to him, "Freddie, there's a revival meeting taking place at Melrose Baptist Church on old Humble Road, and I want you to go with me. There's a preacher there, Dan Vestal, Sr. You come hear Dan Vestal. Please, son, come with me."

Finally, the young man gave in and said, "All right, all right. I'll come." When Freddie walked into the church, dressed like the pimp he had become, he saw his father, his stepmother, and his estranged wife sitting on the front row, waiting for him. But there was no way the proud Houston gang leader was going to sit on the front row of that church. He took his seat in the back instead.

When his dad saw him at the back, he motioned to the others, and they all got up from their places to sit with him. From the moment the music started in that service, Freddie felt something powerful going on. And then Dan Vestal got up to preach, declaring that we are all sinners. We're sinners by birth, sinners by nature, sinners by choice, and sinners by practice. With his open Bible in hand, he declared that all have sinned and fallen short of God's glory, and the wages of sin is death. He spoke passionately about judgment, the cross of Christ, and the need to be born again.

From the time Dan Vestal began to speak, Freddie Gage could sense something stirring in his heart. And then at the end, everyone began singing the invitation hymn, *Just as I am.* Freddie said to himself, *I could never come to Jesus. There's no way I could walk down that aisle.* His dad said to him, "Freddie, go! Go down there. Give your heart to the Lord."

"No!" he replied. "I can't."

Someone whispered something to Dan Vestal, and the evangelist spoke gently into the microphone. "There's a boy here we've been praying for. If he comes to Christ, hundreds of young people will come to God."

Then Dan Vestal left the platform and went down to the back row of the church where Freddie Gage was. Putting his arm on Freddie's shoulder, he said, "Would you like to become a Christian, son?"

"I can't," Freddie said again. "I can't live up to it!"

Vestal replied, "No, you can't live up to it. If you could live up to it, there would be no need of your being saved, would there?" With that, the evangelist closed his eyes and began to pray. Freddie was clutching the pew in front of him tightly, fighting the Holy Spirit as He worked on his heart. Freddie wanted to be saved, but he didn't think he could be saved. He wanted to pray, but he didn't know how to do it or what to say.

Then something happened that changed everything. While Dan Vestal was praying silently over "The Cat," a tear rolled off that preacher's cheek and splashed onto Freddie's hand.

"It scalded my skin like boiling water," Freddie recalled in his book, "and suddenly, I wanted this man's Jesus." He walked down to the front with his wife beside him, and they were both saved that night. His life would forever be changed!

Do you know what I love about that story? Obviously, I love the fact that a derelict from the streets of Houston found life and forgiveness in the Savior, but I also love that Dan Vestal cared about that young criminal. He cared so much, in fact, that he was moved to tears. And one tear touching Freddie's hand made an eternal difference in his life. What if we cared about lost people that much? When is the last time you wept over a soul on the broad road headed for hell? The old axiom is surely true, "People don't care how much you know until they know how much you care."

The Fake News of the enemy whispers as loudly today as it ever has. His mission is the same as it's always been: to steal, kill, and destroy. His strategies are subtle, his lies believable, and his methods individualized to defeat us and keep us from a personal relationship with Jesus. But the truth is this: Satan is a defeated foe! Jesus' death, burial, and resurrection conquered death, hell, and the grave. Jesus has won, and His ultimate victory celebration is on the horizon!

Jesus wants to make an eternal difference in your life and in the lives of your friends and loved ones. He is "not wishing for any to perish but for all to come to repentance" (2 Peter 3:9). It is no coincidence that the last chapter of the last book of the Bible is an invitation to come to Jesus. Look at Revelation 22:17 again:

> "The Spirit and the bride say, "Come." And let the one who hears say, "Come." And let the one who is thirsty come; let the one who wishes take the water of life without cost."

Salvation and the glories of an eternity with Jesus in heaven are available to any and all who will simply "come" to Him in repentance and faith. Jesus said, "the one who comes to me I will certainly not cast out." (John 6:37)

If there is breath in your body, it's never too late to come to Jesus, receive forgiveness, and know that your eternity in heaven is secure. I look forward to seeing you in glory one day!

Conclusion

Are you familiar with the term *subjective truth?* It is truth that resides in the subject as opposed to the object (objective truth). If I say, "Blue is the prettiest color of the seven colors of the rainbow," that is my subjective opinion or subjective truth. You can easily disagree with me because my statement is one of preference, not one of fact, science, or reality. But if I say, "Blue is one of the seven colors in the rainbow," that is a factual truth that resides not in me, the subject, but in the rainbow, the object. Anyone can look at a rainbow and find the color blue. It is objectively there.

In today's modern, progressive society, a society that tries to distance itself from objective, absolute truth, we often hear this dismissive retort, "Well, that's your truth, but it isn't my truth." But genuine truth, by definition, is not a subjective thing. It is a provable fact that exists in the world of reality, not fantasy. When truth becomes possessive and subjective ("my truth"), it moves into the realm of personal opinion—and personal opinions can easily be wrong.

When the Lord created planet earth, He set things up with fixed, absolute truths that govern the physical world. God is a God of order, not chaos and confusion. Seedtime and harvest don't switch places on the calendar from one year to the next. Math, science, horticulture, medicine, and engineering are based on objective realities. Subjective truth surely doesn't cut the mustard when building a fifty-story skyscraper. If you violate sound and proven engineering principles in construction, the results will always be disastrous. You must build, plant, operate, and calculate in accordance with the reality God has established.

Just as we see physical truths and realities at work in our world, we also see spiritual truths at work. These spiritual truths are not subjective. They are objective, absolute, graciously revealed to us in the Bible, and constantly attacked by the devil. For example, the demonic idea that there are many paths to God, as multitudes of people gladly accept, is expressly refuted in Scripture. There is only one way to the Father, and that one way is through His Son, Jesus Christ. Jesus Himself said, "I am the way, and the truth, and the life; no one comes to the Father but through Me" (John 14:6).

In this book, we have covered some of the devil's biggest lies—lies that have horrible and everlasting consequences for those who believe them. We all have family members, friends, neighbors, classmates, workmates, teammates, and those we rub shoulders with on a regular basis who hold to the devil's fake news, thinking it is right. And the only way out of Satan's web of lies is a strong dose of the truth.

As God supernaturally shines the light of truth on the darkness of deceit, spiritual realities begin to come into focus. Subjective spiritual truth (whatever I believe is right) gives way to objective spiritual truth (whatever the Lord says is right), and I can be set free to experience the abundant life of love, joy, and peace found only in Jesus.

I say frequently from the pulpit that God is not the God you want Him to be. He is the God who is. He is not the God of your imagination, the God you wish Him to be—One who does your bidding and turns a blind eye to your sin, selfishness, and rebellion. Oh, no. God is the God who is revealed in Scripture, the God who is Holy, Sovereign, large and in charge. He told Moses at the burning bush, "I AM WHO I AM" (Exodus 3:14). Truly, He is far more wonderful than we can comprehend. His love is unlimited . . . and so is His holiness and righteousness.

In the book of Jeremiah, the Lord says, "Let not a wise man boast of his wisdom, and let not the mighty man boast of his might, let not a rich man boast of his riches; but let him who boasts boast of this, that he understands and knows Me, that I am the LORD who exercises lovingkindness, justice and righteousness on earth; for I delight in these things,' declares the LORD." (Jeremiah 9:23-24)

If we will spend time seeking the One true God through prayer, Bible study, worship, and scriptural meditation, we will get to know the Lord better and better each day. We will grow in our relationship with Jesus and be able to discern good from evil, right from almost right. The devil's lies and subtle deceptions will become evident as we immerse ourselves in the truth that sets us free.

Acknowledgments

I am very grateful to all the people who worked closely with me to get this book to print. In putting together a project like this, it truly takes a village.

My beautiful wife Debbie worked tirelessly in reading, rereading, proofing, and editing the manuscript—and encouraging me to keep going when I hit a snag or a frustration concerning deadlines with the project. She is the best! To be sure, I don't deserve her.

Gabrielle Shannon worked closely with Debbie to proof every page. She is a godsend, and we are so thankful to have her on the From His Heart staff.

My friend Larry Libby did much to get each chapter streamlined and laid out succinctly. This book would not have gotten off the ground without his faithful efforts. I owe him a debt of gratitude.

Casey Shannon and Dr. Larry Nobles, the current and former Executive Directors of From His Heart Ministries, worked behind the scenes to iron out all the logistics in order to get this book to print. I appreciate each of them and their expertise and support.

Esther Fedorkevich and the good people at The Fedd Agency have helped us every step of the way. We are blessed to work with such a wonderful group of dedicated professionals.

The members and staff of First Baptist Church are such a blessing. They encourage me on a daily basis as I endeavor to be a faithful pastor and speak the truth in love. God has been so good to allow me to shepherd this wonderful body of believers who faithfully serve, give, shine, and share to make a difference in this world for Christ.

And most of all, I want to acknowledge and thank the Lord Jesus Christ. He has saved me, blessed me, called me, and enabled me to do the work of the ministry. Since the day I received Him as Savior and Lord (January of 1980), He has been faithful to me. I count it the greatest privilege and honor to serve the King of kings. May He use this book to bless and strengthen the lives of all who read it.

—DR. JEFF SCHREVE
Texarkana, Texas

Loved Reading?

Please reach out to our team at heart@fromhisheart.org
or 903-838-8329 to order in bulk or get a discount.

About the Author

Jeff Schreve became the Pastor of First Baptist Church Texarkana in February of 2003 and founded From His Heart Ministries in late 2004. He previously served on staff at Champion Forest Baptist Church in Houston, Texas. Jeff graduated from the University of Texas at Austin in 1984 with a degree in Business Administration.

After spending twelve years in the business world as a salesman (Landell Manufacturing, Waste Management, Inc., and Nalco Chemical Company), God called Jeff to preach. He earned a Master of Divinity degree from Southwestern Baptist Theological Seminary in December of 2000 and a Doctor of Ministry degree from Southeastern Baptist Theological Seminary in December of 2014.

Jeff is a passionate communicator whose love for the Lord and love for people comes out in every sermon he preaches. He thinks the Christian life is the most exciting life of all. He also thinks being boring is a terrible sin. Pastor Jeff started From His Heart Ministries for the purpose of reaching people around the nation and the world for Christ with the Word of God.

Jeff met his wife, Debbie, in the Singles Department at Champion Forest Baptist Church in 1985. They were married in 1986 and have been blessed with three wonderful daughters, two sons-in-law, two precious granddaughters and three adorable grandsons.

Additional Resources

by Jeff Schreve

BOOKS

- *The Promise of Eternity: From The Sermon Series "Forever and Ever: The Reality of Eternal Heaven and Eternal Hell"*
- *Life Interrupted: How to Face a New Normal*
- *Now That's Encouraging: Strength for the Day*
- *Runaway Emotions: Why You Feel the Way You Do and What God Wants You to Do About It*

BOOKLETS

- *God's Answer to Your Anger*
- *How to Be Sure You're Going to Heaven*
- *When Victims Meet Victory*
- *When Fear Meets Faith*
- *I Still Do* (Jeff and Debbie Schreve)
- *Sticks & Stones: What to Do When the Going Gets Tough*
- *Hitting the Bull's-Eye: Knowing and Doing God's Will*
- *When You Don't Like Yourself*
- *Not Guilty*
- *In the Face of Discouragement*
- *Real Revival*
- *Strong Faith for Tough Times*
- *Unveiling the Mystery of Prayer*

- *Are You Worried About Money?*
- *Before You Say "I Do"*
- *How Near is the End?*
- *The Divine Helper: Uncovering the Mystery of the Holy Spirit*
- *The Lord's Army: How to Be a Good Soldier of Christ Jesus*
- *Turn Out the Lights: When God Pulls the Plug on a Nation*
- *When God Doesn't Make Sense*
- *The ABC's of the Christian Life*

From His Heart Ministries is the Christian evangelical and teaching media outreach ministry of Pastor Jeff Schreve, and reaches hundreds of thousands of people on over 800+ radio stations and thousands of TV outlets as well as several digital platforms across America, and is also available in 180+ countries around the world.

CONNECT WITH JEFF HERE

Number: 903-838-8329
Email: heart@fromhisheart.org
Instagram: @fromhisheartministries
TikTok handle: @fromhisheart
Facebook: From His Heart Ministries
X: @jeffschreve

His daily live call-in radio podcast, Real Truth for Today,
can be heard each weekday morning on www.afr.net.